Current
CONTROVERSIES

Attacks on Science

Other Books in the Current Controversies Series

| Attacks on Science

Lisa Idzikowski, Book Editor

WITHDRAWN

GREENHAVEN
PUBLISHING

Published in 2022 by Greenhaven Publishing, LLC
29 East 21st Street, New York, NY 10010

First Edition

Articles in Greenhaven Publishing anthologies are often edited for length to meet page
requirements. In addition, original titles of these works are changed to clearly present
the main thesis and to explicitly indicate the author's opinion. Every effort is made to
ensure that Greenhaven Publishing accurately reflects the original intent of the authors.
Every effort has been made to trace the owners of the copyrighted material.

Cover image: shuttermuse/Shutterstock.com.

Library of Congress Cataloging-in-Publication Data

Names: Idzikowski, Lisa, editor.
Title: Attacks on science / Lisa Idzikowski, book editor.
Description: First edition. | New York : Greenhaven Publishing, 2022. |
   Series: Current controversies | Includes bibliographical references and
index. | Audience: Ages: 15 | Audience: Grades: 10–12 | Summary: "The viewpoints
in this title consider the impacts of attacks on science, whether these attacks can be
stopped, and how they can be prevented. It also examines the role of the internet
in propagating and legitimizing these attacks"— Provided by publisher.
Identifiers: LCCN 2020051526 | ISBN 9781534507944 (library binding) | ISBN
   9781534507920 (paperback) | ISBN 9781534507951 (ebook)
Subjects: LCSH: Science—Social aspects—Juvenile literature. |
   Science—Political aspects—Juvenile literature. | Science—Public
   opinion—Juvenile literature.
Classification: LCC Q175.5 .A88 2022 | DDC 306.4/5—dc23
LC record available at https://lccn.loc.gov/2020051526

Manufactured in the United States of America

Website: http://greenhavenpublishing.com

Chapter 2: Are Attacks on Science Harmful to Society?

Yes: Attacks on Science Are Harmful to Society

Science has helped society in many ways since historical times. A vital service in modern times is prevention of outbreaks and pandemics. The only way to achieve this is to understand evolution and to implement its scientific precepts. Attacks on teaching evolution must be prevented and stopped.

No: Certain Regulations of Science Is Appropriate

Chapter 4: Are Attacks on Science a Recent Phenomenon?

Foreword

"Controversy" is a word that has an undeniably unpleasant connotation. It carries a definite negative charge. Controversy can spoil family gatherings, spread a chill around classroom and campus discussion, inflame public discourse, open raw civic wounds, and lead to the ouster of public officials. We often feel that controversy is almost akin to bad manners, a rude and shocking eruption of that which must not be spoken or thought of in polite, tightly guarded society. To avoid controversy, to quell controversy, is often seen as a public good, a victory for etiquette, perhaps even a moral or ethical imperative.

Yet the studious, deliberate avoidance of controversy is also a whitewashing, a denial, a death threat to democracy. It is a false sterilizing and sanitizing and superficial ordering of the messy, ragged, chaotic, at times ugly processes by which a healthy democracy identifies and confronts challenges, engages in passionate debate about appropriate approaches and solutions, and arrives at something like a consensus and a broadly accepted and supported way forward. Controversy is the megaphone, the speaker's corner, the public square through which the citizenry finds and uses its voice. Controversy is the life's blood of our democracy and absolutely essential to the vibrant health of our society.

Our present age is certainly no stranger to controversy. We are consumed by fierce debates about technology, privacy, political correctness, poverty, violence, crime and policing, guns, immigration, civil and human rights, terrorism, militarism, environmental protection, and gender and racial equality. Loudly competing voices are raised every day, shouting opposing opinions, putting forth competing agendas, and summoning starkly different visions of a utopian or dystopian future. Often these voices attempt to shout the others down; there is precious little listening and considering among the cacophonous din. Yet listening and considering, too, are essential to the health of a democracy. If controversy is democracy's lusty lifeblood, respectful listening and careful thought are its higher faculties, its brain, its conscience.

Current Controversies does not shy away from or attempt to hush the loudly competing voices. It seeks to provide readers with as wide and representative as possible a range of articulate voices on any given controversy of the day, separates each one out to allow it to be heard clearly and fairly, and encourages careful listening to each of these well-crafted, thoughtfully expressed opinions, supplied by some of today's leading academics, thinkers, analysts, politicians, policy makers, economists, activists, change agents, and advocates. Only after listening to a wide range of opinions on an issue, evaluating the strengths and weaknesses of each argument, assessing how well the facts and available evidence mesh with the stated opinions and conclusions, and thoughtfully and critically examining one's own beliefs and conscience can the reader begin to arrive at his or her own conclusions and articulate his or her own stance on the spotlighted controversy.

This process is facilitated and supported in each Current Controversies volume by an introduction and chapter overviews that provide readers with the essential context they need to begin engaging with the spotlighted controversies, with the debates surrounding them, and with their own perhaps shifting or nascent opinions on them. Chapters are organized around several key questions that are answered with diverse opinions representing all points on the political spectrum. In its content, organization, and methodology, readers are encouraged to determine the authors' point of view and purpose, interrogate and analyze the various arguments and their rhetoric and structure, evaluate the arguments' strengths and weaknesses, test their claims against available facts and evidence, judge the validity of the reasoning, and bring into clearer, sharper focus the reader's own beliefs and conclusions and how they may differ from or align with those in the collection or those of classmates.

Research has shown that reading comprehension skills improve dramatically when students are provided with compelling, intriguing, and relevant "discussable" texts. The subject matter of these collections could not be more compelling, intriguing, or urgently relevant to today's students and the world they are poised to inherit. The anthologized articles also provide the basis for stimulating, lively, and passionate classroom debates. Students who are compelled to anticipate objections to their own argument and identify the flaws in those of an opponent read more carefully, think more critically, and steep themselves in relevant context, facts, and information more thoroughly. In short, using discussable text of the kind provided by every single volume in the Current Controversies series encourages close reading, facilitates reading comprehension, fosters research, strengthens critical thinking, and greatly enlivens and energizes classroom discussion and participation. The entire learning process is deepened, extended, and strengthened.

If we are to foster a knowledgeable, responsible, active, and engaged citizenry, we must provide readers with the intellectual, interpretive, and critical-thinking tools and experience necessary to make sense of the world around them and of the all-important debates and arguments that inform it. We must encourage them not to run away from or attempt to quell controversy but to embrace it in a responsible, conscientious, and thoughtful way, to sharpen and strengthen their own informed opinions by listening to and critically analyzing those of others. This series encourages respectful engagement with and analysis of current controversies and competing opinions and fosters a resulting increase in the strength and rigor of one's own opinions and stances. As such, it helps readers assume their rightful place in the public square and provides them with the skills necessary to uphold their awesome responsibility—guaranteeing the continued and future health of a vital, vibrant, and free democracy.

Introduction

> *"Science is the greatest collective endeavor. It contributes to ensuring a longer and healthier life, monitors our health, provides medicine to cure our diseases, alleviates aches and pains, helps us to provide water for our basic needs—including our food, provides energy and makes life more fun, including sports, music, entertainment and the latest communication technology. Last but not least, it nourishes our spirit."*
>
> *— "Science for Society,"*
> *UNESCO*

Since the fourteenth century, science has been understood as the state of knowing: knowledge as distinguished from ignorance or misunderstanding. Most likely, science means different things to different people. Some may think of science as the exploration of space or the undersea world. Some may think it has to do with discovering new medicines or medical advances. Others may understand it as a way of explaining the biological diversity of the planet or how elephant herds organize their behaviors. And some may even envision a "mad scientist" stirring a bubbling pot of noxious vapors.

It is curious to think of individuals who have a skepticism regarding science or who attack the practitioners or theories of science. Especially since, according to a 2019 Pew Research survey, almost three-quarters of Americans believe that "science has, on balance, had a mostly positive effect on society." And over 80 percent feel that future developments in science will benefit society in the years to come. So how do these statistics fit in with the idea of science being under attack? Why are attacks on science harmful? Should they be prevented? Or should questioning of science and scientists be considered legitimate practice?

Attacks on science have happened in the past and continue today. In 1633, famous Italian physicist and astronomer Galileo Galilei was accused of heresy by the Roman Catholic Church. After his trial, then reciting and signing a formal statement, Galileo was put under house arrest. Why? All because he upheld the teachings of another scientist. Copernicus argued that the sun, not Earth, was the center of the universe, and Galileo agreed.

More than two hundred years later, Charles Darwin agonized over publishing his great theory of evolution in *On the Origin of Species* (1859). He knew it would be controversial. He knew its ideas would trouble many, including his own wife. But he also believed it had to be delivered to the world. He had observed, gathered, experimented, and finally brought everything together by writing his grand theory. Equally grand is that another scientist, Alfred Russel Wallace, also had his own version of evolution, a near copy of Darwin's ideas ready to unleash upon the world.

Evolution and its ideas have been attacked by many for a long time. Some misguided individuals demand that creation science be given equal importance. Even though, according to a 2014 Gallup poll, roughly four in ten American adults believe in creationism, saying God created humans, almost all scientists steadfastly accept and adhere to evolutionary theory. This is appropriate and necessary. Researchers agree that understanding evolution is the path forward when it comes to producing medical advancement, and most critically in the race against antibiotic resistance.

Once can witness the modern-day effects in a lack of scientific belief or outright attack on scientists during the coronavirus pandemic. In the early days of the outbreak of COVID-19, there may have been differing views among experts. How could it have been otherwise? The world was dealing with a pathogen that was brand new to humans. But as experimental evidence came together, most experts agreed on the severity of the virus, its devastating effects, and the most effective methods of combatting it until a vaccine could be developed and delivered to everyone. Politics played a large role in the way Americans trusted or mistrusted science during the pandemic. Europeans generally believe that the United States handled the pandemic poorly. According to a 2020 Pew Research survey, "In 11 of the 13 countries surveyed, half or more say the US has done a *very* bad job dealing with the coronavirus outbreak."

A serious question remains whether attacks on science should be prevented, or if these attacks might prove to be harmful. An obvious answer is "yes." Any individual alive during 2020 experienced a historical event that has wide implications concerning attacks on science. Anyone paying attention during 2020 saw President Donald Trump and his supporters attack various scientists, doctors, data collectors, politicians, and many others.

What did these attacks accomplish? Most medical professionals would agree that these attacks did nothing to lessen the pandemic in the United States. One of the highest profile medical experts, Dr. Anthony Fauci, director of the National Institute of Allergy and Infectious Diseases, repeatedly worked to combat erroneous information about the pandemic. "I have been on the airways, on the radio, on TV, begging people to wear masks," Dr. Fauci said. "And I keep talking in the context of: Wear a mask, keep physical distance, avoid crowds, wash your hands, and do things more outdoors versus indoors." Of course, there are many other examples one can explore that argue the case against science and scientists coming under attack.

On the flip side, are there any legitimate instances when scientists or science should be scrutinized or regulated? Some scientists think so! Back in 2014, Britain's premier theoretical physicist, Stephen Hawking, told the BBC that simpler forms of artificial intelligence (AI) had been beneficial to humanity, but he worried that complex forms could be developed that might surpass human capabilities. "It would take off on its own, and re-design itself at an ever increasing rate." And he worried that "humans, who are limited by slow biological evolution, couldn't compete, and would be superseded." Not all scientists share Hawking's views. At the same time, Hawking was not alone in his thinking, and others share his worries still today. Just as there are various instances where science should not be attacked, there are numerous reasons besides the worry about AI gone wild that science and scientists benefit from peer review and watchfulness.

How faithfully should we adhere to science, and how do we know what to believe when the science is too complicated for most of us to understand? Should we trust politicians, who increasingly have strong opinions about science, even though they might not understand it themselves? The current debate surrounding this interesting topic can be understood by reading and contemplating the viewpoints compiled in *Current Controversies: Attacks on Science.*

CHAPTER 1

Can Attacks on Science Be Scientifically Legitimate?

Overview: Analyzing Good and Bad Science

Nick Frost

Nick Frost is an author who writes on a variety of issues.

Ask anyone who works at Kinova—or any other robotics company focused on developing technology to increase human capability, for that matter—and they'll tell you how rewarding their work can be. They'll tell you how challenging, and interesting, and stimulating, and how much unadulterated fun it can be.

But they'll also, at times, tell you how irksome it can be.

Not because of the work itself—rather, because of how, within the field of robotics, the literal life-changing significance of the technology they develop is often overshadowed by seemingly impressive feats that smack of being more gimmicky than anything else.

And that's with no disrespect to the obviously skillful individuals who work on robots that can mimic human behaviour in cute or funny ways. But when 1,069 dancing robots setting a Guinness World Record for the most robots dancing simultaneously is a more "newsworthy" headline, and given more traction to grab the public's collective attention than scientific breakthroughs that will impact humanity in a major way, something is incredibly amiss.

Bad Science Under the Microscope

Speaking with regards to the broader scientific community as a whole, why is it that so much bad science (or, as it's sometimes called, "junk science") continues to pervade society?

Before we answer that, let's first clarify what we mean by this decades-old term. Junk science doesn't just have to apply to the kind of con artistry we see from shysters-turned-TV pitchmen, who offer

"The Good, the Bad and the Ugly: Outlining the Difference Between Good and Bad Science," by Nick Frost, Kinova. Reprinted by permission.

up false hope to unhealthy individuals in the form of "miracle cures" with zero scientific merit—though, that's certainly one extreme.

Rather, the term encompasses anything that passes itself off as legitimate science, but is ill-intentioned. Either it has an ulterior motive seeking to counteract credible scientific facts or has little to no real significance to the human population.

This could include several things: studies paid for by companies looking to alter their public perception, results that create a cloud of misconception around things already proven in order to serve politically motivated agendas, or even breakthroughs in which a scientist will skew and manipulate results to make a name for him- or herself.

Sadly, as long as there are scientists willing to act in less legitimate manners, and people who either willfully ignore the merits of good science, can't tell the difference or upon whom doubts are easily cast, bad science will continue to have an audience.

How Does One Spot the Differences Between Bad Science and Good Science?

First things first, just to be clear, our definition of good science is any type of science that works constructively towards helping humans understand and function in the world around them.

Spotting the differences can sometimes be tricky, particularly when bad science is presented in a way that makes it appear legitimate.

One might automatically assume that a study receiving news coverage might be a surefire way to determine the legitimacy of scientific information. But, then again, the news sometimes tells us that things (take the health effects of kale, for example) are both good and bad for you.

Certainly, a great deal of media coverage on scientific research is presented in a sensationalistic way with eye-catching headlines made to draw the reader in (many of whom won't read past the eye-catching headline or, at most, the article's lede). Part of this, as accomplished science writer Julia Belluz notes, can be attributed to the lack of true science journalists that exist in that industry's current landscape, where jobs are being cut on an almost monthly basis. Writers who don't fully understand the research they're writing about are limited in their ability to present it and, therefore, are more susceptible to overselling the juicier points to attract clicks.

The easiest way to determine the legitimacy of scientific research is to read any study you come across with a critical eye and ask questions:

- What is the source of the research—a university, an independent study, a medical journal or something else?
- What kind of language does the research use—is it affirmative or speculative?
- What methods were used and under what conditions was the sample group tested?
- Are the results peer reviewed?
- Are the results replicable?

Ms. Belluz—a very reliable source in the scientific journalism community—provides a good checklist of even more questions that you run through when questioning the merits of anything scientific.

There are thousands upon thousands of examples of both good and bad science, historically speaking, but here are just a handful to illustrate our point:

Good Science...

Darwin's Theory of Evolution (1859): Renowned naturalist Charles Darwin, the father of modern evolutionary theory, lays out the basis for all future study of evolution, stating, among other things, that all life descends from a common ancestor and species develop through the "natural selection" of inherited traits.

MMR Vaccine Discovered (1971): American microbiologist Maurice Hilleman, regarded as "the most successful vaccinologist in history," combines the measles, mumps and rubella vaccines he's known for discovering to create the first vaccine using live virus strains, almost entirely wiping the diseases out.

SpaceX Rockets to Success (2006–present): Though Elon Musk will likely be known for far more wildly imaginative inventions when all's said and done, his work thus far in space exploration has seen his Dragon rocket become the first commercial vehicle to dock with the International Space Station, and his company, SpaceX, holds the record for a rocket engine with the highest thrust-to-weight ratio.

JACO Robotic Arms Launch (2009): Eight years ago, Kinova brought one of its most significant inventions to life: JACO, a six-axis robotic manipulator arm with a three-fingered hand. Since then, JACO has played key roles in improving the lives of humans with reduced upper-body mobility and, just this year, was used by Airbus to begin testing its capabilities in helicopter avionics.

Bad Science...

Cold Fusion Goes Cold (1989): After many failed attempts at replication, electrochemists Martin Fleischmann and Stanley Pons' alleged breakthrough on a nuclear reaction at room temperature—and the hopes of cheap, renewable energy—is debunked. (Though, many are still trying to this day.)

Schön Scandal (2004): German physicist Jan Hendrik Schön, once prominent in the physics community for work with single-molecule semiconductors, has 24 charges of misconduct laid against him and his doctorate stripped for manipulating experiment data.

MMR Vaccine Falsely Linked to Autism (1998): British gastroenterologist Andrew Wakefield publishes a research paper falsely linking MMR to the autism. While his claims were discredited and he's since been banned from the UK medical register, the damage has been irreversible, as some parents still refuse to vaccinate their kids.

Fellow Scientists Will Correct Errors of Other Scientists

Seth Shostak

Seth Shostak is a senior astronomer at the SETI Institute.

Are you among those who doubt that climate change is caused by humans? You have company: Half of the American populace is on your side. For them, anthropic causes of global warming are an illusion or possibly a hoax. But that teeming horde doesn't include many climate scientists. Only 13 percent of these experts dispute that climate change is largely wrought by man.

What about biological evolution, an idea that's now 157 years old? Do you think your presence on this planet is the consequence of the adaptation and change of species with time? If not, there's no need to feel marginalized by your skepticism. Two-fifths of your countrymen figure that *Homo sapiens* somehow arose in its present form only 10,000 years ago. They consider it laughable to suggest that an undirected process could have produced something as wonderful and complex as themselves. However, you won't find many biology professors in that crowd.

Perhaps you suspect that vaccines cause autism? Or that GMOs are bad for your health? What about that clumsy government cover-up of an alien saucer crash near Roswell, N.M.? Large fractions of the public consider these ideas—which run contrary to mainstream science—at least plausible.

So what's going on here? What's happened to the credibility of the white-lab-coated brainiacs who were once the final authority on how everything worked? Today, many in the public regard scientists as having motives that go beyond merely sussing out nature's machinery. They are perceived as having an agenda that threatens lifestyles as often as it improves them.

"Science Under Attack," by Seth Shostak, The Trustees of Princeton University, March 22, 2017. Reprinted by permission.

Has science become unreliable, closed-minded, or possibly even malicious? Is the public wrong in occasionally regarding science with raised eyebrows, especially when it intrudes in the most personal of ways by admonishing people that major trouble is afoot if they don't riddle their infants with a volley of vaccines or curtail their love for large cars?

Intrusions into daily life have set up science as the bad boy for those with a liking for old-fashioned agriculture, natural medicine, or bulldozing coal from the wilds of Wyoming. The result is a significant hostility to science or, if you're partial to expansive phraseology, an "attack on science." This attack is as unsurprising as belly fat. Science is in the business of explaining things, and as its range of explanation continually expands, so will the societal consequences.

This is a modern phenomenon, as our regard for science has shifted considerably in the past seven decades. After World War II, science mutated from an egghead enterprise to a major engine of society. Even apart from proving itself indispensable for vanquishing present and future enemies, research was seen as a relentless promoter of a better life. What followed was a decades-long honeymoon in which scientists looked beautiful from every angle. In the 1950s, nuclear power ("our friend, the atom") promised to supply us with electricity at a price too cheap to meter. On TV, avuncular doctors, sheathed in de rigeur lab coats, confidently assured viewers that certain brands of cigarettes were actually good for them.

Today, the haloed scientists of the past have given way to less benign models. Scientists are no longer the ultimate authorities. A prime example of this can be found in the brouhaha over childhood vaccinations. Roughly one in 10 people suspect that these vaccines cause autism. This has motivated parents (often wealthy and well educated) to avoid inoculating their kids and has been one of the few science topics discussed, albeit inaccurately, by presidential candidates. It has become a major public issue, rather than a matter of personal principle, because vaccines—like self-driving cars— offer their greatest societal benefits only if everyone participates.

There is overwhelming evidence that discredits any link between vaccines and autism. Nonetheless, large numbers of parents choose to rank their intuition (or the testimony of movie stars) above peer-reviewed research, irrespective of the direct and occasionally lethal consequences. They distrust the scientists, who in their eyes have somehow morphed from saints to devils.

How can one understand such a monumental decline in authority? One obvious explanation is to recognize that scientists— like everyone—are fallible. They make mistakes, and occasionally cheat by manipulating or fabricating data. When this happens, when pointy-headed professors turn out to be as reliable as Ford Pintos, their transgressions become a useful cudgel for those who think that scientists are goring their ox.

But at the risk of sounding self-serving, science seldom stays wrong for long. Science autocorrects. Nothing pleases a researcher quite so much as demonstrating that a competitor has made an error, offering the delicious opportunity to set the record (and the textbooks) straight. If your conclusions are faulty, the first one to challenge you surely will be another scientist.

Because of this self-correction, it's a weak argument to suggest—as anti-vaxxers and climate-change deniers often do—that the science asserted by large numbers of researchers is mistaken. That's a precarious position, and the odds against it being right are long. It's one attack on science that has little chance—no more than slingshots against a castle wall.

But here's another, more subtle explanation for the dulling of science's luster: a widespread unease about where it's taking us. When the Renaissance was getting underway, no one could imagine the long-term changes that the newly invented discipline of science could foster. It sowed seeds that flowered in unexpected ways.

Consider a modern example: A century ago, when physicists were developing quantum mechanics to describe the seemingly preposterous behavior of atoms, few outside academia had obvious reason to care. Indeed, even the scientists themselves were unsure that their work was any more consequential than doing the Sunday crossword. As recently as 1940, the British mathematician G.H. Hardy declaimed that relativity and quantum mechanics were "almost as useless as the theory of numbers." And at the time, the last was quite useless.

But that's changed. Anyone with a cellphone owns a device that would have been impossible to build without an understanding of the non-intuitive conduct of very small bits of matter. Quantum mechanics is everywhere.

The frequent delay between research and benefit is a strong argument against politicians who feel that research must always have an obvious practical goal. Sen. William Proxmire became famous (and eventually notorious) for his Golden Fleece Award, a finger-pointing exercise directed against federally funded science he considered frivolous. Quantum mechanics certainly would have qualified.

But delay or not, there's no doubt that the public now recognizes that the future really is being fashioned in the lab, and that research into artificial intelligence or genetics may result in discomfiting scenarios. Are white-collar workers destined to lose their jobs to ever-smarter robots? Will their grandchildren inevitably begin life as designer babies? For some people, today's scientists are busily clearing the path to tomorrow's nightmare.

Inevitably, as the scope of science has grown, it has shed the benign regard in which it was held. Modern physics was once far removed from the mind of the average person, and thoroughly innocuous—until it produced the atomic bomb. Today's science touches subjects that are big in anyone's budget: defense, health care, and the environment.

Despite these understandable worries, I believe that much of the contemporary distrust of science is motivated not by its occasional inaccuracies or even its unpredictable and possibly sinister outcomes, but by a very human resistance to its practitioners.

This isn't because scientists wear black hats, but because they deal in dark arts. If you disagree with science or its findings, it's a tough slog to take it on. After all, researchers are armored with intellect, status, tenure, and subject matter that's about as comprehensible to the uninitiated as the Dead Sea Scrolls.

As middle-school kids love to lament, modern science is hard. In the 19th century, there were discoveries lying around like fallen fruit just waiting to be collected by the observant and thoughtful. You could become an expert in nearly any research area with little more than an above-average intellect and a week in a decent library. This was the era of gentlemen scientists with time on their hands—"natural philosophers" sporting tweedy jackets rather than sheepskins on the wall.

That era definitely is past tense. To prove the existence of the Higgs boson required a machine, the Large Hadron Collider, that took $9 billion and more than a decade to build. About 10,000 specialists were involved. No member of the landed gentry ever would have made that discovery.

Indeed, the author list on one of the seminal papers describing the uncovering of the Higgs had 5,154 names on it. That's more text than many research papers of a century ago, and is a good indicator of the cumulative nature of science. Knowledge builds on itself. Newton could not have understood what the Higgs discoverers found, despite the fact that his brain was undoubtedly more supple than most of theirs.

This is in dramatic contrast to other societal endeavors, such as the arts. Books, plays, and music still are largely the work of individuals, and these individuals need not stand on the shoulders of their predecessors for much more than inspiration. Would anyone say that a modern composer, say Elton John, has totally eclipsed Mozart thanks to two centuries of progress in music? Is Wolfie no longer worth a download? Even movie-making, which today employs teams as large as those doing particle physics, is—aside from its greater technical finesse—hardly changed from its past.

Would you really argue that contemporary films are fundamentally more captivating than those of the '30s and '40s?

Science obviously is different. As the easy stuff is mastered, cutting-edge research leads to deeper complication. As a result, it becomes less easily grasped by non-experts. While even high school students of two generations ago could appreciate the concept of atoms and picture what "splitting the atom" might mean, how many among the citizenry of today command enough science to appreciate string theory, or what problem it's trying to solve?

The result is that those whose lives are forcibly altered by science understandably can regard it as an enemy—and its practitioners as enemy troops. The research establishment is sometimes seen as a society of bullies, emboldened by fancy degrees.

Researchers themselves often are surprised by this tendency to, in their view, blame the innocent. Scientists argue that they are entirely agnostic when reporting on the safety of GMO foods or the effects of coal-fired power plants. If there's a fight about these things, it doesn't include any dog of theirs. The researchers are simply calculating the odds. They never promised that their efforts would be agreeable, entertaining, interesting, useful, or beautiful. The citizenry doesn't need to like what science tells it. In this regard, it's unlike nearly any other activity you can name.

In addition, scientists generally are nonplussed by accusations of cover-up or hidden knowledge imposed by fearful governments. As anyone who has worked in research knows, science is very bad at keeping secrets.

So where does this battle lead? Personally, I think it's destined to fade with time. Millennials surely have a better understanding than their predecessors of the truth that basic research is the midwife of future technology. And just about everyone is sympathetic to the promise of improved technology—be it in their cars, in medicine, entertainment, or personal electronics. This spawns a soft undercurrent of support for science. We want the goodies, so we'll ante up for the R&D.

True, this support could be likened to a religion: In our hunger for the technology, we take the science on faith. I suspect that rather few people find the existence of the Higgs boson interesting or comprehensible enough to discuss at cocktail parties. But they have little issue with the fact that billions in tax dollars (admittedly, mostly European tax dollars) were spent to track it down.

There seems to be a historical buy-in that, because we want the fruit, we're willing to invest in the orchard—or at least in a small grove. The budget for the National Science Foundation is 0.2 percent of the federal budget. But that expenditure hasn't caused the citizenry to reach for their lanterns and pitchforks (although it must be noted that the amount spent on non-defense research has stagnated for the past dozen years).

So is there really a good reason to think that the attack on science is damaging our research efforts and our future? In the short term, you could argue there is. The frustrating reluctance to confront the existential problem of climate change could come back to bite us in a big way. However, and as contrary as it might sound, the failure to vigorously address this issue might be cured by a worsening of the problem itself. As pundits enjoy noting, America generally is unenthusiastic about making hard choices on problems until they're as obvious as vaudeville humor. With 16 out of 17 of the hottest years on record being experienced in the scant time since the new millennium began, climate change is one problem that may become dramatically manifest very soon, provoking some serious action.

But what about the long term? Has science had its heyday in America? A perennial lament is that the public has very little understanding of science—not just the facts, but also how it works and how it decides if something is likely to be true or not.

Judging from the phone calls and emails I receive every day, you might think this lament has legs. I'm astounded by how many people are willing to accept that any bright dot of light in the night sky is convincing proof that alien spacecraft are sailing overhead, or that the Egyptians used extraterrestrial consultants to build the pyramids.

Disconcerting indeed, but I suspect these experiences are largely a selection effect: I hear only from the people who choose to get in touch with me. And what's different today is that they can. The internet allows everyone to engage with anyone.

What I believe is more relevant than the funky phone calls is the fact that the fraction of college freshmen who intend to major in science or engineering is substantial. Indeed, it was about one-third in 1995, and since then has increased by about 10 percentage points. This group is far more diverse with regard to sex and ethnicity.

As important as these metrics are, I derive the greatest encouragement from the way science is seen by our culture. Being a nerd is now a compliment, and not—as it once was—a one-way ticket to social ostracism. STEM education is valued by parents and sought for their children. TV shows and movies—which once portrayed the scientifically adept with derision—now frequently make them the heroes.

The attack on science, insofar as such aggression is real, should be resisted. But it seems to me, when I look at the prestigious role models that scientists—despite their complicated jobs—have become, I figure that "the kids will be alright." The offensive against science is one attack that can be repulsed. I'm counting on the youth.

Legitimate Scientific Scrutiny Is Necessary and Should Be Expected

Elisabeth Pain

Elisabeth Pain is the editor for the European branch of the American Association for the Advancement of Science.

Science and scientists are under constant scrutiny. Most of that scrutiny is healthy. It's good when scientists challenge each other and discuss issues as they work together—sometimes taking opposite sides—to disentangle the true and enduring from the fleeting and flawed. Governments must guarantee that resources are used wisely, experiments are done ethically, and the benefits of research are transferred to society. The public has a right to question how science may impact their lives and whether scientists can be trusted. Accepting fair criticism, then, is an essential professional duty.

But not all criticism is fair or made in good faith. Even scientists sometimes cross the line: Peer reviews turn vitriolic, questions to speakers turn condescending, and scientific disputes turn personal. Scientists and their work may attract unwanted public attention, too, and gratuitous online nastiness. In recent years, an increasing number of scientists in politically and ideologically sensitive fields have become targets of hate e-mails, death threats, campaigns aimed at discrediting them and their entire field, and legal battles.

Some scientists may be surprised when this happens and find such experiences deeply unsettling. While it's important not to spend too much time or effort anticipating such events, a bit of preparation can be useful. When they find themselves on display in an unfair and unflattering way, scientists should take a deep breath, calm down, sort scientific arguments from personal attacks, and calculate an appropriate response—or just let it go.

Savage Peer Reviews

Whether it's because they are overworked, lack training, vested in a particular theory or methodology, or just having a bad day, sometimes scientists write what Cornell University psychologist Robert Sternberg calls "savage reviews." "A savage review is one that is either personalized—in other words, the criticisms are of the persons rather than of the works—or the criticisms are of the works but the language is excessive … for the gravity of the sins," Sternberg explains; he estimates that he has received a dozen savage reviews during his career.

It's easy to get upset, but you shouldn't, Sternberg says. "One of the things you need to do as you become more advanced in the field is just to shrug these things off and not let them bother you." Try not to take offense. "Just ignore the personal part in the language. Just see if there is anything in the review that you can use to improve your work."

Public Rows About Science

Things get trickier when intense criticisms are made publicly. "You're best off, when that happens, just giving a straight answer, and the hell with it," Sternberg says. When he was interviewing for his first university job, "someone asked what I thought was a sort of stupid and condescending question in a job talk I gave, and being 24 years old and naive, I gave a snappy answer," he says. "I later just found out that the guy was the chair of the search committee, so that was kind of the end of that job."

A few years ago, cognitive psychologist Axel Cleeremans of the Université Libre de Bruxelles attempted to replicate a classic study by John Bargh of Yale University, in which some participants were primed, without realizing it, with concepts associated with old age. Bargh's study found that they walked more slowly from the exam room than subjects who had not been so primed. Cleeremans's group found that they could not replicate the result unless the experimenters were told to expect a slower walking pace.

The failed replication attempt, which was published in *PLOS One* in 2012, was picked up by science journalist Ed Yong at his Not Exactly Rocket Science blog and attracted a lot of attention. Bargh responded with a post on his own blog, at *Psychology Today*, where he spelled out the errors that he believed the Cleeremans group made. The post, titled "Nothing in their Heads," used a tone Bargh later told *The Chronicle of Higher Education* that he now regrets; it has since been taken down. Yong described the post, in a subsequent blog post of his own, as "a mixture of critiques of the science within the paper, and personal attacks against the researchers, *PLOS ONE*, the journal that published it, and me, who covered it." Harsh words flew in Bargh's direction, too, as Bargh's critics accused him of ad hominem attacks and attacked him in turn, often via anonymous comments.

"I was hurt by the things that were said, not just in the article, but in Ed Yong's coverage of it," Bargh told *The Chronicle*. He still feels "frustration and sadness at how he's been treated," *The Chronicle* reports; some scientists in the article describe him as "a victim of scientific bullying" and the controversy over priming as "a referendum on one man." Attempts by *Science Careers* to contact him were unsuccessful.

There have always been scientific controversies of course, and they have not always been civil. What has changed is how visible they are. Such disputes once led to intense private correspondences, shouting matches at academic meetings, or series of letters to journals with several months' lag time between. Today, such disputes can be viewed in all their glory, instantly, by anyone with an interest. They leave a record that can stay online forever or until someone decides to take it down.

Being publicly challenged can be difficult, says Cleeremans, who found Bargh's comments "a little bit insulting" and felt he had to respond to intense scrutiny to his work. As Cleeremans sees it, the most important thing is to dissociate criticism of the science from personal attacks on the scientist. Scientific criticism suggests "that you are onto something … definitely important enough that people feel that they should … position themselves in terms of agreeing or disagreeing with what you've found, so it is already a mark of recognition." Should your study fail to replicate, you can replace it with a new hypothesis, note another interesting effect, or correct the study, he adds. "That's the process of science."

When responding to criticism, it's also important to weigh your words. "When it's all taking place in public like that, it's difficult because of course what you say is instantly retweeted … so you have to exert a degree of restraint and care when you speak."

Scientists often take it personally, but they shouldn't, Cleeremans says. "Anybody can genuinely make an error or genuinely interpret results in a certain way but be proven wrong later on, that doesn't change anything to who you are as a person." Should you be on the receiving end of personal attacks, "my advice would be to, in general, sort of ignore it [because] everybody understands that such attacks are not scientific arguments in any sense."

Online Harassment

"For the longest time, the only people reacting to academic research were either academics or people who were very interested in a particular field," says Whitney Phillips, a media studies scholar at Humboldt State University in Arcata, California. But "things are … so visible now that anybody … can say something on a blog and then suddenly find themselves on the receiving end of lots of weird commentary."

There are lots of different kinds of nasty behaviors online, and how they are perceived largely depends on the receiver, Phillips says. Online nastiness can go all the way from potentially offensive general comments to personal attacks directed at you. Sometimes it can even "reac[h] the legal criteria for harassment, so someone is not just saying rude things to you but is … potentially even threatening you or trying to wiggle their way into your life," Phillips says.

Women and minorities are disproportionately exposed to online antagonism and may also be more sensitized because they already confront it in real life, Phillips says. At its worst, online harassment can affect your ability to work, and it can require a great deal of emotional fortitude to continue, she adds. "The real worry is that you would have ... people from historically underrepresented groups in the sciences ... deciding that they want to leave the field ... [at a time when] there needs to be more diversity in the sciences."

Phillips suggests limiting the power of "Internet trolls"—and encouraging meaningful conversation with the rest of the public—by deleting anything they (the trolls) post on your blog, banning them from your site, and using word filters. Try not to get sucked in, as what they want most is a response and an audience, she says. Also, seek support from your peers. "The problem with online harassment is that it makes you feel isolated, and it can sometimes make you question your sanity that you are reacting really strongly to these different comments." Talking to people will help you realize you are not the only one and have done nothing wrong, Phillips explains.

In the Firing Line

Ideologically or politically sensitive fields like climate change, environmental protection, genetically modified organisms, animal research—even evolution—are more likely to attract public attacks intended to intimidate, distract, and harm the reputation of individual scientists and, often, their entire field. While such ideology-driven critics have long existed (especially in the United States) their fervor and the weapons at their disposal have increased in the recent years, says Michael Halpern, who is program manager at the Center for Science and Democracy of the Union of Concerned Scientists (UCS) in Washington, D.C.

Michael Mann, a climate scientist at Pennsylvania State University, University Park, has experienced many attacks since his "hockey stick" curve was published in the 2001 report of the

Intergovernmental Panel on Climate Change. Mann has since become an outspoken defender of climate science and been the victim of many vilifying media reports, campaigns aimed at discrediting him, the misuse of open-records laws, e-mail hacking (in the so-called "Climategate"), and threats to his and his family's safety.

Such attacks can be "very stressful, it can take a lot of a scientist's time. … Unfortunately if their institution doesn't support them, it's potentially very expensive" in legal costs, says Lauren Kurtz, executive director of the Climate Science Legal Defense Fund. It can detract from your ability to do research, Kurtz adds. There also is a danger that it will derail your career, especially for young scientists who don't have the security of tenure, Mann writes in an e-mail. "[T]here is always a fear that your colleagues and bosses (chairs, deans, provosts, presidents) will believe the scurrilous accusations made against you."

Scientists under such scrutiny should "first and foremost, just do good work," Kurtz says. "A good scientist … will always prevail in the end." Also, when entering the debate and communicating your research to the public, "you do need to be conscientious about what you're saying and making sure that you're communicating in an effective way."

Prepare

Hopefully, most scientists will never be seriously impacted by such unwelcome exposure, but everyone should prepare by becoming aware of the risks and giving a bit of thought as to how they should respond, Halpern says. UCS has issued a booklet detailing what to do (and what not to do) in a broad range of situations. Concerned scientists might also want to talk to their universities and departments to see how much (and what kind of) institutional support they could count on.

Over the past few years, the American Geophysical Union has offered legal advice at annual meetings. The American Chemical Society has reported extensively on attacks against scientists in

Chemical and Engineering News. The Climate Science Legal Defense Fund provides legal support to scientists so they can focus on their research. The fund and UCS put researchers in touch so they may provide each other with emotional support and practical advice.

One mistake scientists commonly make is to "look to any sort of criticism as they would in a scientific context and try to answer every single question that comes their way, when sometimes those kinds of questions are just meant to distract or take time or create material that can be taken out of context later," Halpern says. And "sometimes, it's better not to engage the attacker directly." A safer place for scientists to respond is their own website, where they can explain what their research is about and provide some context while staying in control of the conversation, Halpern says. Resist the tendency to attack back or say things in frustration or anger, he adds.

Scientists should also recognize that there is a limit to what they can achieve, says Marcel Kuntz, a research director and fundamental plant biologist at the National Center for Scientific Research in the Laboratory of Plant and Cell Physiology in Grenoble, France. Kuntz entered the public debate about genetically modified organisms (GMOs) in France after observing what he calls a growing tendency by French public authorities to distort scientific findings for political ends and after reading an alarmist article in his local newspaper, he says. At first, he tried to take part in adversarial debates. But he gave that up, realizing that "I won't be able to express what I want to express as a scientist, I am obliged to refute lies with political ends during the whole debate, and hence I enter a game where I myself become a political militant," he says.

Now Kuntz, who has added writing journal articles reviewing the state of GMO research to his portfolio of academic activities, talks to the press and runs a blog on the issue—which has, of course, attracted offensive commentaries. His aim is to use his scientific knowledge and rhetorical skill to explain what is known, what is not known, and what political interests are at play—and then let the public decide. Scientists should communicate, "but without absolutely wanting to impose their views," Kuntz says. They should also be aware that combining academic activities in such diverse fields dilutes your work, which can be counterproductive for your career, especially for young researchers who are still in the race for permanent positions.

Truth Will Win Out

However upsetting it may feel to be a target of public attacks, "in some ways it's almost a badge of honor, because you're doing work important enough to attract the ire of these ideologically motivated groups," Kurtz says. She recommends that scientists, first of all, take a deep breath and recognize that other scientists have come up on the other side. The importance of fighting back unjustified attacks goes beyond your public reputation and the field's credibility, Halpern says. "When you push back against attacks, you create space for researchers to be able to continue to ask tough questions and pursue contentious research."

Mann says he has always had faith in the principle that truth will win out, and at this point in his career he feels that it has, he writes in his e-mail. "[D]on't allow yourself to be sidetracked," he writes. "[F]ight back when necessary to defend your science against bad faith attacks, but the best defense here is a good offense. [J]ust keep on doing good science and you'll be fine."

Science and Religion Should Operate Independently

Georg Scholl

Georg Scholl is the director of marketing and communications at the Humboldt Foundation.

Researchers may believe in theories, but seldom in miracles. Thus conflicts with religion may seem inevitable, whereby questions of faith already keep researchers occupied amongst themselves.

Some researchers believe in economic models for predicting developments in the world economy and international markets. Some believe that one day someone will manage to prove the string theory, which could be along the lines of general operating instructions for the universe and everything that happens in it. The famous American astronomer Carl Sagan believed that sooner or later humanity would receive signals from intelligent extraterrestrial life forms, and spent decades listening to outer space with the help of enormous radio telescopes. And his compatriot, the highly-decorated astrophysicist Thomas Gold of Cornell University, believed that oil is not actually a fossil fuel based on biomass but a metabolite of bacteria living in the earth's crust that process hydrocarbon.

Anyone who looks at science as being essentially a business of rationality, hard facts and empiricism underestimates the role of fixed ideas and intuition, not to mention the conviction that you are on the right path even if you cannot prove it. However, in the end, faith is supposed to turn into proven knowledge. It is not enough just to believe in the existence of extraterrestrial life—it all depends on what you are able to prove. This consensus amongst researchers sounds trivial. But it is the root of conflicts with religions that are based on faith without evidence. In the world

"Research—A Question of Faith," by Georg Scholl, Alexander von Humboldt-Stiftung/Foundation. Reprinted by permission.

of religion miracles are certainly possible, in the world of research they are not. Here we are dealing with the maxim of the Scottish philosopher David Hume: "No testimony is sufficient to establish a miracle, unless the testimony be of such a kind, that its falsehood would be more miraculous than the fact which it endeavours to establish." The fact that some researchers are prepared to believe in divine miracles nonetheless does not make the conflict any clearer.

Searching for the God Module

The urge to plumb the depths of the inexplicable and miraculous leads science almost in passing—and sometimes even intentionally—onto religious territory. Progress in modern brain research, for example, has made the topic of faith even more fascinating to science. Researchers push Tibetan monks or Catholic nuns into a magnetic resonance tomograph to investigate which regions of the brain are active during meditation or prayer. The discovery of an increase in the blood supply to the front temporal lobe even prompted the American neuropsychologist V.S. Ramachandran to declare this region of the brain to be a so-called God module. This region of the brain, which seems to be responsible for religious experience, also works the other way round. If the respective area is stimulated with magnetic waves or affected by an epileptic attack, this can trigger a sense of transcendental enlightenment or religious experience in subjects and patients.

In the last resort, is God perhaps nothing more than a storm of neutrons in the human brain? Ramachandran chooses not to answer this question. Like many neurologists he is not simply prepared to exchange belief in God for belief in the brain. After all, the existence of a God module does not contradict the existence of God. Perhaps creation has specifically earmarked it as the receiver designate of spiritual messages and experiences? Another theory explains mankind's predisposition to the religious by evolution: Selection has favoured people with the relevant area of the brain because religious experience can strengthen social bonds within a community.

The Brain as Belief Engine

Another explanation as to why human beings both wish to and have to believe in something is provided by the British developmental biologist Lewis Wolpert. His reasons for the positively compulsive human search for answers not only explain the drive for religion and belief in miracles, but for research as well. Wolpert sees the brain as a belief engine: In the search for understanding it drives human beings at least to believe, even if they do not actually know—be it in God, astrology, extraterrestrials or string theory.

According to Wolpert, the reason for this is the human ability to link cause and effect. In the dim and distant past, it was this that allowed us to invent the first primitive tools. Without this insight, even combining a biface with a simple stick for a handle to invent an axe would not have been possible. This ability set off a cognitive chain reaction. Once you have understood the connection between cause and effect you cannot stop searching for reasons why the world is as it is. Once you have understood that you only have to rub two sticks together vigorously to create fire, you want to know the causes of other things, such as disease and death. But it proved impossible to apply the principle of "no effect without a cause" to strokes of fate of this kind without resorting to the supernatural. When our ancestors reached the limits of their understanding they almost inevitably came to the conclusion that an invisible God must be responsible—a solution that was so compelling, and has remained so for many to this day, that a lot of societies developed it quite independently.

However, with every puzzle that research manages to solve the scope for supernatural explanations is reduced. Since Darwin and the triumph of science the claim to universal validity made by religious dogma has diminished constantly. Eventually people will be asking whether there is a God at all if everything can be explained without him. The defensive reactions of the religious are concomitantly strong. In the spectacular debates between creationism and evolutionary theory in the USA, religious adherents of intelligent design, who consider Darwin's teaching fallacious and the Bible to be the definitive tool for explaining the origins of the world, are pitted against radical atheists like the biologist Richard Dawkins, who reject any thought of a divine plan of creation as complete rubbish.

Faith without evidence is the aspect of religion that fires on opponents like Dawkins. If being religious means believing in something without evidence, anything is justifiable—no points of argument, no evidence, the only justification being that one simply believes in it, as Dawkins claims in his international bestseller, *The God Delusion.*

Who Stands Where on the Issue of Faith?

Dawkins does not only argue with the representatives of religion. One of his adversaries is the geneticist Francis Collins, for example. The former head of the National Human Genome Research Institute publicly champions the harmony of science and faith and openly declares his belief in God, the virgin birth and the resurrection of Jesus. Other scientists, like the palaeontologist and evolutionary biologist Stephen Jay Gould, preach that science and religion are two completely independent worlds existing next to each other on an equal footing. The adherents of this view argue that the naturalism of evolutionary theory leaves ample room for the idea that God created the universe but then left it to natural history to take its course in the context of the laws he had determined—which did not stop him from interfering here and there.

Long before the current debate on science and religion started in the USA, the issue of God and his role in the world view of research was discussed with reference to Albert Einstein and his theory of relativity. But as the chief witness for scientists who believe in God, Einstein is not much use. His famous remark about God not playing dice was not so much a profession of faith as an allegory indicating that the universe, too, must be governed by fixed laws. In one of Einstein's letters written in 1954, which was only discovered recently, he wrote to the philosopher Eric Gutkind, "The word God is for me nothing more than the expression and product of human weaknesses, the Bible a collection of honourable, but still primitive legends which are nevertheless pretty childish. No interpretation no matter how subtle can (for me) change this." Nevertheless, Einstein did not describe himself as an atheist and claimed, "What I see in Nature is a magnificent structure that we can comprehend only very imperfectly, and that must fill a thinking person with a feeling of humility. This is a genuinely religious feeling that has nothing to do with mysticism."

Faced with the enormous puzzles of their respective disciplines, many researchers would undoubtedly subscribe to this opinion. Similarly, there is agreement that in the search for truth it is quite legitimate and, indeed, may even be helpful to start out from a position of disinterested belief. However, whether we really have the activities of bacteria to thank for oil, whether it is possible to predict the u-turns in the economy, or whether the answer to the mysteries of the universe is a mathematical world formula or the existence of a higher being—in the end, for most researchers this is bound to be a question of evidence rather than faith.

President Trump Disregards Science on All Fronts

Andrew Rosenberg

Andrew Rosenberg directs the Center for Science and Democracy for the Union of Concerned Scientists.

Eighteen months ago, I wrote a blog called the *ABC's of Sidelining Science* by the Trump Administration because there were so many examples of this administration's disregard for scientific process and evidence that I could readily/easily fill out the alphabet. I thought of updating my alphabet-of-wrongdoing at the end of 2019, but then thought it would be more helpful/interesting/ etc. to instead utilize a great resource that Merriam-Webster, the dictionary people, put online called "Trending Words in the News." While these are cool words that appear in news stories, my intent is to use them in descriptions of recent science-related actions by the Administration. Here we go.

Braggadocio

Earlier this year, President Trump gave a speech on his environmental "accomplishments" full of claims about all the great things he was doing for the environment. More recently, Trump again touted his great concern about climate change. Suffice it to say that this was pure braggadocio, as I pointed out in a previous blog. In fact, air pollution has gotten worse during this administration, reversing a thirty-year trend of improving air quality. The US played a negative, blocking role at the recent climate change meetings in Madrid. And a host of other impacts show that the administration's environmental record is nothing to brag about.

"Nine Trendy Words for the Trump Administration's Attacks on Science," by Andrew Rosenberg, Union of Concerned Scientists, January 2, 2020. Reprinted by permission.

Probity

The Bureau of Land Management (BLM) is the manager of vast areas of federal lands that are held in the public trust. That means they are managed on behalf of all Americans, not just those who seek to exploit their natural resources. But William Pendley, the acting head of the BLM, has massive conflicts of interest that keep him beholden to the exploiters not the people. To make matters worse, many of the BLM's Washington staff have been required to relocate to Grand Junction, CO, or quit the agency, even though their jobs require them to work with other agencies and Congress in DC. And the new headquarters in Colorado is in the building that is home to Chevron, a state oil company and a natural gas company, all of whom exploit public lands. All this leads to a real question of the probity of BLM leadership.

Insidious

The Environmental Protection Agency (EPA) has continued to try to finalize a new rule restricting the science the agency will consider in protecting public health and safety, the primary mission of this agency. The proposed rule and recent supplemental proposal would mandate that the agency principally rely on scientific studies where all of the underlying raw data, computer code, models and other information are fully publicly available. This despite more than 600,000 overwhelmingly critical comments on the proposal, largely from the science community, but also from Congress, concerned about excluding important research based on medical information that can't be made public. While the agency has performed no analysis of the impact, cost, or consequences of imposing such a rule, nor even clearly stated and analyzed what problem they are trying to solve, the proposal has far-reaching impacts for public health. It would exclude many studies of the population-level impacts of pollution, known as epidemiological studies. And it would allow the EPA Administrator, not scientists, to decide what scientific information could be included, by giving she/he the power to exempt studies from the requirement. Even the agency's own Science Advisory Board can't seem to find any redeeming features for this proposal. The impact is truly insidious, potentially setting back public health protection for decades.

Egregious

Without any justification or guidance, the President has ordered that one-third of all federal advisory committees be terminated. This despite the fact that these committees provide expertise from outside of government for very little cost (mostly just meeting travel). Apparently, this administration doesn't want external advice from scientists and other experts, with Administrator Wheeler proposing a "don't call us, we'll call you" approach just recently. At the EPA they have gone even further by declaring that scientists with agency research grants have conflicts of interest and may not serve on advisory boards but industry-based scientists and consultants are free from conflicts and may provide advice. This is such an egregious manipulation of the process that even a federal appeals court recently questioned if it had any basis at all.

Dastardly

In addition to the relocation of BLM staff to Colorado for flimsy reasons, the Department of Agriculture has gotten into the act by reassigning two whole programs to move out of DC. Secretary Sonny Perdue announced that the Economic Research Service and the National Institute of Food and Agriculture must move. Never mind that the programs will lose most of their staff. In fact, that seems to be the point of the exercise in the first place, even though it is illegal to transfer employees in order to get them to quit. A truly dastardly move that hurts farmers, consumers, and the country for no purpose.

Kangaroo Court

Beyond simply cutting advisory panels, this administration has also gone out of its way to pack what should be panels of independent scientists with industry-tied members who are likely to give the answer the administration wants. A key case in point is the Clean Air Scientific Advisory Committee (CASAC), the group tasked under the Clean Air Act with advising the agency on air pollution. But, in the Trump EPA, the panel is led by a consultant to industry who consistently maintains that a more "rigorous" test of cause and effect must be met before reducing the level of pollutant exposure. The majority of experts in the field view that test as inappropriate. If such as standard were applied, public health protections would be scaled back on pollutants such as fine particulate matter, which is responsible for more than 100,000 deaths annually in the US. An expert panel for reviewing the science concerning the health impacts of particulate matter pollution was dismissed. But, with a little help from the Union of Concerned Scientists, those experts decided to meet anyway and provide the advice the agency didn't want to hear. So now the record clearly shows that the science supports reducing particulate matter pollution. Despite this, the official CASAC couldn't reach a decision after holding a kangaroo court review of the science.

Quid Pro Quo

The industry that has benefited the most from Trump's policies and reductions in public health, safety, and environmental protections is unquestionably the fossil fuel industry. Many of the political appointees in agencies from the EPA to Department of Energy and the Department of the Interior spent much of their careers lobbying on behalf of industry. And the administration's positions denying the reality of climate change and withdrawing from the Paris climate accord have been at the behest of fossil fuel companies and their lobbying groups. So, what did they get in return for their support? Opening of public lands to oil and gas production. Potential leasing in the Arctic National Wildlife Refuge. And leasing of more offshore areas for oil drilling despite intense public resistance. For their support they got access to resources despite the public interest—the essential quid pro quo.

Mendacious

We would all like to think that our government makes every effort to protect children, especially from threats to their development.

Unfortunately, there are many examples where this administration had the opportunity, the science, and the tools to take actions that would clearly benefit children's health. But they failed. One of the most egregious, and also mendacious, concerns restrictions on the use of the pesticide chlorpyrifos. Long-term scientific studies have shown the harm this chemical can cause to kids, particularly those in farming communities with high risk of exposure. But the EPA has failed to act despite the evidence, contrary to the facts. The courts have stepped in demanding that the EPA consider the evidence and justify why such a dangerous chemical should continue to be used, but still the agency failed to act. Mendacity is not an argument for refusing to act, in other words.

Stymie

There has been a lot of recent talk about "forever chemicals" like Poly Fluorinated Alkyd Substances (PFAS). The new movie *Dark Waters* is publicizing the issue and none too soon. There are known health effects even at low exposure levels. But military families and other communities are being exposed to extremely high levels. Unfortunately, neither the EPA nor the Department of Defense has stepped up. And Congress has so far not required action. Needed protections for public health have been stymied. But it shouldn't be that way. The risk is clear and widespread across the country. More research, more technology and more protections all are needed. Not in five years, but now.

I know this list could go on for pages and pages. But I hope the point is made. These actions are not what the government should do. Not how policies should be made. We need to listen to the science advice, be focused on serving the public interest, and put health and safety at the forefront for everyone in this country. To make that a reality, everyone's voice needs to be heard—not just industry, not just those supporting one political view, but everyone. Because we are the public. Speak up and stand up for science.

Energy Companies Obstruct Climate Science in Various Ways

Climate Investigations Center

The Climate Investigations Center is a group of individuals that monitor organizations and individuals trying to delay the implementation of sound environmental policies.

Internal documents and conversations from the fracking lobby, revealed this week in HuffPost, shine new light on a ten year old public relations campaign front group called Energy in Depth. Documents show this front group is designed explicitly to exist without the fingerprints of its fossil fuel funders, giving the oil industry the "ability to say, do and write things that individual company employees cannot and should not."

This reporting reveals how climate denial remains a key oil industry strategy in spite of their efforts to clean up their image. These shrouded attacks on climate science and solutions, attacks on lawmakers, scientists, lawyers and advocates stand in stark contrast to the seemingly desperate efforts of Exxon and their brethren to retain "social license," gain credibility on climate change and distance themselves from their legacy of climate science denial.

Let's define "climate denial" up front, as we did years ago in a *Guardian* interview for a story about Edelman PR: "Our definition of denial is anyone who is obstructing, delaying or trying to derail policy steps that are in line with the scientific consensus that says we need to take rapid steps to decarbonize the economy." Simple enough. It goes beyond just denying that global warming exists.

"Exxon and Friends Still Funding Climate Denial and Obstruction Through IPAA, FTI, Energy in Depth," Climate Investigations Center, December 20, 2019. https://climateinvestigations.org/exxon-and-friends-still-funding-climate-denial-and-obstruction-through-ipaa-fti-energy-in-depth/. Licensed under CC BY 4.0 International.

HuffPost's reporting shows that Exxon is a member of the Independent Petroleum Association of America (IPAA), an oil and gas industry trade association whose online assets include "news" sites like Energy in Depth (EID) that spew climate denial and attacks on scientists, journalists, advocates, and lawyers. IPAA acts as a pass through, bundling corporate members' cash that's funneled to the firm FTI Consulting, which created and manages sites like EID. An ExxonMobil spokesperson, responding to questions from the HuffPost reporter, tried valiantly to keep the veil in place, saying, "Your questions are better addressed to EID or IPAA."

IPAA's Long History of Denial

The IPAA has a long history of funding and proliferating misinformation on climate change, a legacy that continues to this day. IPAA was named as a potential funder of the infamous multi-million dollar "uncertainty" campaign detailed in the 1998 Global Climate Science Communications Plan, an effort organized by API, Exxon, Chevron, Southern Company and assorted libertarian extremists.

Potential funding sources were identified as American Petroleum Institute (API) and its members; Business Round Table (BRT) and its members; Edison Electric Institute (EEI) and its members; Independent Petroleum Association of America (IPAA) and its members; and the National Mining Association (NMA) and its members. Potential fund allocators were identified as the American Legislative Exchange Council (ALEC), Committee for a Constructive Tomorrow (CFACT), Competitive Enterprise Institute, Frontiers of Freedom and the Marshall Institute.

The IPAA fact sheet on climate change released that same year has some pretty alarming climate denial claims—some even more extreme than the Global Climate Coalition was pushing at the time, and includes references to Fred Singer's Leipzig Declaration and the Imperial Oil DRI/McGraw Hill study on carbon taxes. IPAA also blame termites and volcanoes—basically everything but fossil fuels—for altering the atmosphere more than fossil fuels:

> "Consider this: the largest source of greenhouse gas may be termites, whose digestive activities are responsible for 10 times more production of CO2 than burning fossil fuels."

> "So, since human-related CO2 is only a small portion of total atmospheric CO2, measures taken to limit it will have little or no measurable effect on overall emissions into the atmosphere. More importantly, there is still no evidence that CO2 emissions are warming the earth's atmosphere. And we have no proof that man's impact makes a difference at all."

By 2008, the IPAA had a more nuanced fact sheet on climate change, but still emphasized uncertainty and denial,

> "…no climate change policy action should discard the question of science. Too often, recent arguments for action discard the uncertainties of today's understanding of global climate science. Global climate science is an emerging field, one that changes as the tools to model it improve."

They Know Better…

The Washington Post revealed that in a June, 2019 presentation at an IPAA meeting, influential energy lawyer Mark Barron said the "ship has sailed" on using climate science denial as the first line of defense. Instead, Barron advocated lobbying Congress for climate legislation that benefits the oil and gas industry. He drew a sharp contrast between the industry's former attacks on climate science and a more recent nuanced approach. He told the oil and gas executives and lobbyists gathered at the meeting sponsored by fracking giants Halliburton, Schlumberger and Oxy that they should be ready to talk about global warming, as long as they position fossil fuels as the solution. Despite this, HuffPost reporting shows that Barron's audience, the IPAA and its members, are still deploying on climate denial and attacks on scientists through projects like EID and other web organs.

Funding Front Groups—FTI and Energy in Depth

IPAA describes Energy in Depth as the industry's lead "rapid response platform" for the fracking industry. IPAA created Energy in Depth (EID) shortly after the environmental impacts from the fracking boom began to make national headlines. IPAA member Exxon/XTO was one of EID's first funders.

Internal IPAA Board documents, published by HuffPost, describe the purpose of the project:

"The main focus of EID has evolved into addressing the "Keep It in the Ground" movement." (Keep It in the Ground refers to activists and scientists working to keep new fossil fuels from being extracted and burned, commensurate with the conclusion by international scientists that we simply cannot burn even a percentage of known and potential fossil fuel reserves if we want to keep global temperatures from rising to dangerous levels.)

Funding for EID comes directly from unnamed oil and gas corporations like Exxon, Halliburton, Schlumberger, Oxy, Marathon Oil, and is funneled through IPAA, which funds the Energy in Depth project on an annual basis.

According to IPAA budget documents, the EID campaign costs more than $2 million per year, representing about one fifth of IPAA's total budget, second only to "Salaries and Benefits" in scale.

Big question: What puzzles us is how IPAA is classifying this expense to the IRS. This $2M plus annual payment to FTI does not appear, as required by law, on the IRS 990 form filed by IPAA under "Independent Contractors" "that received more than $100,000 in compensation from the organization." Perhaps IPAA can provide an explanation.

The Real Story of Energy in Depth

Colleagues at DeSmog have been watching Energy in Depth from the beginning, when it was launched to blunt attention to the rapid spread of fracking ten years ago and concerns from community members, lawmakers, journalists and activists.

IPAA's Jeff Eshelman described the genesis and purpose of the group in a 2017 IPAA retreat. The IPAA funding of over $2M a year to FTI/Energy in Depth is spent on five sub-campaigns, meant to undermine the public's understanding and support of climate and environmental protections:

- EID Climate exists "to counteract the "Keep It in the Ground" movement's newest strategy to use climate change as a weapon to silence dissent and shut down American energy production." The website pushes back on litigation against oil and gas companies.
- EID Health is a "rapid response program" to counter studies linking oil and gas drilling and production to health impacts.
- Endangered Species Watch is meant to blunt the Federal Endangered Species Act and is described as "disseminating news, regulations and issue alerts to member companies, affiliated industries and policy makers."
- Energy Tax Facts defends tax subsidies for the fossil fuel industry.
- Fossil Fuel Divestment Campaign advocates against movements asking universities and pension funds to divest from fossil fuels.

FTI has carved out a specialty in aggressive attacks on foes of the oil and gas industry, doing the dirty work that oil corporations would not want their brands tied to in public. An FTI "Techical Paper" report presented at a 2014 Brazilian oil industry conference describes Energy in Depth's purpose pretty bluntly, stating that the web asset provides the **"ability to say, do and write things that individual company employees *cannot and should not*."** (emphasis added)

The actual work of running EID is contracted out by IPAA to FTI Consulting, a massive global PR and consulting firm. Here are a few individuals we know are connected to the Energy in Depth project and have written themselves into the wrong side of history:

Matt Dempsey, a Managing Director at FTI, manages Energy in Depth and lists himself as an editor for WesternWire, another front group run for Western Energy Alliance, another oil trade association like IPAA. Dempsey and a colleague were recently recorded by a lawyer for EarthRights International who called them out for being agents of Exxon, and pretending to be journalists. Exxon is a defendant in the Boulder Colorado lawsuit that EID and WesternWire have tried hard to malign. Dempsey used to work for Senator James Inhofe.

Steve Everley is an FTI Managing Director of Strategic Communications and a senior advisor on the Energy in Depth project. *Inside Climate News* ran a lengthy rebuttal to the work Everley did to trash their actual journalism on fracking in 2014.

Spencer Walrath is actually an FTI employee (Director, Energy & Natural Resources at FTI Consulting Inc.) but pretends to be an journalist on Energy in Depth. He graduated from the University of Northern Iowa in 2012. Spencer's FTI job was announced in his college newsletter.

Katie Brown, PhD, who now works for FTI out of Belgium, was a major part of Energy in Depth while working for FTI in Washington, DC, until a couple years ago. [A] 45 slide Powerpoint presentation from 2014 by Brown lays out the IPAA-FTI-EID connection and details all their work to undermine regulations on ozone, groundwater protection, methane emissions and more. (Brown's PhD is in English, btw, and she is or was working on a book on James Joyce…congratulations, but how does that PhD apply to an energy front group website besides using good grammar?)

More EID Denial

- FTI's Energy in Depth Climate front group spends most of its pixels trying to trash climate lawsuits, promoting natural gas as a climate solution, and attacking science implicating methane's role in climate change. Methane, a super greenhouse gas and the main component of "natural gas," leaks from fracking fields in vast quantities making the current natural gas supply much dirtier fuel than it used to be before fracking became a thing. This point was recently illustrated nicely with FLIR images by the *New York Times*, and news of [a] Exxon gas well leak which released more methane in a few weeks than many countries emit in a year.

- Each of the EID sub-campaigns employ tactics common to climate deniers, like attacking climate models, denying the impact of methane from fracking, repeating debunked myths about a global pause in warming, and claiming that "one in six climate and earth scientists" think human's impact on climate change is "little or none."
- Most recently, Spencer Walrath wrote a piece in EID going after a peer reviewed scientific study on ocean acidification and the companies connected to the carbon dioxide that has acidified the ocean, the science of which is even harder to deny than climate change.
- And this post by Katie Brown, PhD, at EID (https://www .energyindepth.org/even-lawyers-who-empathize-with -ags-goal-say-climate-rico-campaign-setting-dangerous- precedent/) uses sham science and Wikipedia links to attack calls for accountability for companies like Exxon.

EID "Experts"

On the EID Climate website, the list of experts includes people like Craig Richardson, president of the coal-funded, climate- denying Energy and Environment Legal Institute. Richardson has called climate change a communist plot.

Other experts include Horace Cooper, who is listed as a senior fellow at the National Center for Public Policy Research, an organization that has received $445,000 in grants from Exxon over the past two decades including several grants earmarked for climate work.

Cooper is also a Fellow with the preeminent climate science denial group the Heartland Institute. Heartland has held a number of gatherings dedicated to outright climate science denial.

Heartland was also heavily funded by Exxon until they dropped them after 2006. The Mercer Family stepped in in 2008 and has given Heartland upwards of $6.7M from 2008-2017. In 2018, this grant appears to have been moved through Donors Trust.

FTI Work for Other Industries with Legal and Political Problems

In 2019, court documents revealed FTI was running opportunities for Monsanto on RoundUp and GMO fights, alternately posing as journalists and attacking journalists, complete with an FTI campaign spreadsheet of steps taken to undermine and intimidate journalist Carey Gillam.

Most recently, FTI produced a report on health care for a front group attacking "Medicare for All" proposals by politicians.

IPAA Lobbying with Climate Denial Under Trump

IPAA is a significant lobbying arm of the oil industry, spending 1.4 million on lobbying in 2018. Freedom of Information Act requests have revealed emails from IPAA lobbyists to key political appointees in the Department of the Interior, showing an ignorance of basic climate change information and a willingness to disregard climate science when it gets in the way of oil and gas production.

In one set of emails, IPAA lobbyist Samantha McDonald asked DOI appointees to reduce protections on an endangered species of beetle. A key reason IPAA protested the beetle's protected status?—because its projected decline was based in part on climate change science. McDonald directly questioned the viability of climate change models, but not before admitting she is "not too familiar" with the 30 year old UN Intergovernmental Panel on Climate Change (IPCC). As proof that the preeminent scientific body studying climate change in the world could not be trusted, she cited a Google search and a random *Forbes* article. McDonald wrote to DOI appointee Vincent DeVito in 2017:

"All modeling is done using the Fifth Assessment Report of the Intergovernmental Panel on Climate Change. While I am not too familiar with this organization or their work, I did some searching and found this *Forbes* article discrediting the IPCC, citing irresponsible science practices (intentionally manipulating data, suppressing legitimate opposing arguments, etc.). This may be something to look into and push back on, since most of the climate changes threat analysis in the SSA is based on this work."

In spite of her lack of science background, IPAA's McDonald would go on to testify on endangered species law, and the beetle would eventually be "downlisted" by the Trump administration as reported by the *Washington Post*.

In sum, the Energy in Depth project is entirely consistent with the 30 year campaign by the oil industry to avoid being regulated for environmental harm caused by their products—climate change, air and water pollution. This covert effort contradicts oil industry leaders' anxious attempts to portray a greener, climate friendly business model in recent years. We can see right through it, but the aim is clear. Between Barron, the lawyer's comments and IPAA's front group Energy in Depth, the fossil fuel industry clearly is trying to play it both ways—opposing climate action while pushing natural gas as a solution and trying to benefit from whatever climate policies do come to pass and keep drilling away unchecked. All the while refusing to treat the global climate crisis like the real and present danger that it is. While IPAA lobbyists may try to play good cop in meetings on the Hill, they are actually leaning on old fashioned attacks on science to delay and distort any serious attempt to address climate change.

CHAPTER 2

Are Attacks on Science Harmful to Society?

Overview: Science Enhances Humanity

Valentí Rull

Valentí Rull is a senior researcher at the Spanish National Research Council and former director of the Botanic Institute of Barcelona.

Science is valued by society because the application of scientific knowledge helps to satisfy many basic human needs and improve living standards. Finding a cure for cancer and a clean form of energy are just two topical examples. Similarly, science is often justified to the public as driving economic growth, which is seen as a return-on-investment for public funding. During the past few decades, however, another goal of science has emerged: to find a way to rationally use natural resources to guarantee their continuity and the continuity of humanity itself; an endeavour that is currently referred to as "sustainability."

Scientists often justify their work using these and similar arguments—currently linked to personal health and longer life expectancies, technological advancement, economic profits, and/or sustainability—in order to secure funding and gain social acceptance. They point out that most of the tools, technologies and medicines we use today are products or by-products of research, from pens to rockets and from aspirin to organ transplantation. This progressive application of scientific knowledge is captured in Isaac Asimov's book *Chronology of Science and Discovery*, which beautifully describes how science has shaped the world, from the discovery of fire until the 20th century.

However, there is another application of science that has been largely ignored, but that has enormous potential to address the challenges facing humanity in the present day education. It is time to seriously consider how science and research can contribute to education at all levels of society; not just to engage more people in

"The Most Important Application of Science," by Valentí Rull, EMBO Press, August 18, 2014. Reprinted by permission.

research and teach them about scientific knowledge, but crucially to provide them with a basic understanding of how science has shaped the world and human civilisation. Education could become the most important application of science in the next decades.

More and better education of citizens would also enable informed debate and decision-making about the fair and sustainable application of new technologies, which would help to address problems such as social inequality and the misuse of scientific discoveries. For example, an individual might perceive an increase in welfare and life expectancy as a positive goal and would not consider the current problems of inequality relating to food supply and health resources.

However, taking the view that science education should address how we apply scientific knowledge to improve the human condition raises the question of whether science research should be entirely at the service of human needs, or whether scientists should retain the freedom to pursue knowledge for its own sake—albeit with a view to eventual application. This question has been hotly debated since the publication of British physicist John D. Bernal's book, *The Social Function of Science*, in 1939. Bernal argued that science should contribute to satisfy the material needs of ordinary human life and that it should be centrally controlled by the state to maximise its utility—he was heavily influenced by Marxist thought. The zoologist John R. Baker criticised this "Bernalistic" view, defending a "liberal" conception of science according to which "the advancement of knowledge by scientific research has a value as an end in itself." This approach has been called the "free-science" approach.

The modern, utilitarian approach has attempted to coerce an explicit socio-political and economic manifestation of science. Perhaps the most recent and striking example of this is the shift in European research policy under the so-called Horizon 2020 or H2020 funding framework. This medium-term programme (2014-2020) is defined as a "financial instrument implementing the Innovation Union, a Europe 2020 flagship initiative aimed at securing Europe's global competitiveness." This is a common view of science and technology in the so-called developed world, but what is notable in the case of the H2020 programme is that economic arguments are placed explicitly ahead of all other reasons. Europe could be in danger of taking a step backwards in its compulsion to become an economic world leader at any cost.

For comparison, the US National Science Foundation declares that its mission is to "promote the progress of science; to advance the national health, prosperity and welfare; to secure the national defence; and for other purposes." The Japan Science and Technology Agency (JST) states that it "promotes creation of intellect, sharing of intellect with society, and establishment of its infrastructure in an integrated manner and supports generation of innovation." In his President's Message, Michiharu Nakamura stated that, "Japan seeks to create new value based on innovative science and technology and to contribute to the sustained development of human society ensuring Japan's competitiveness."[1] The difference between these declarations and the European H2020 programme is that the H2020 programme explicitly prioritises economic competitiveness and economic growth, while the NIH and JST put their devotion to knowledge, intellect, and the improvement of society up front. Curiously, the H2020 programme's concept of science as a capitalist tool is analogous to the "Bernalistic" approach and contradicts the "liberal" view that "science can only flourish and therefore can only confer the maximum cultural and practical benefits on society when research is conducted in an atmosphere of freedom."[2] By way of example, the discovery of laser emissions in 1960 was a strictly scientific venture to demonstrate a physical principle predicted by Einstein in 1917. The laser was considered useless at that time as an "invention in the search for a job."

The mercantilisation of research is, explicitly or not, based on the simplistic idea that economic growth leads to increased quality of life. However, some leading economists think that using general economic indicators, such as Gross Domestic Product (GDP), to measure social well-being and happiness is flawed. For example,

Robert Costanza, of the Australian National University, and several collaborators published a paper in *Nature* recently in which they announce the "dethroning of GDP" and its replacement by more appropriate indicators that consider both economic growth and "a high quality of life that is equitably shared and sustainable."[3]

If the utilitarian view of science as an economic tool prevails, basic research will suffer. Dismantling the current science research infrastructure, which has taken centuries to build and is based on free enquiry, would have catastrophic consequences for humanity. The research community needs to convince political and scientific managers of the danger of this course. Given that a recent Eurobarometer survey found significant support among the European public for scientists to be "free to carry out the research they wish, provided they respect ethical standards," it seems that a campaign to support the current free-science system, funded with public budgets, would likely be popular.

The US NSF declaration contains a word that is rarely mentioned when dealing with scientific applications: education. Indeed, a glance at the textbooks used by children is enough to show how far scientific knowledge has advanced in a few generations, and how these advances have been transferred to education. A classic example is molecular biology; a discipline that was virtually absent from school textbooks a couple of generations ago. The deliberate and consistent addition of new scientific knowledge to enhance education might seem an obvious application of science, but it is often ignored. This piecemeal approach is disastrous for science education, so the application of science in education should be emphasised and resourced properly for two reasons: first, because education has been unequivocally recognised as a human right, and second, because the medical, technological and environmental applications of science require qualified professionals who acquire their skills through formal education. Therefore, education is a paramount scientific application.

In a more general sense, education serves to maintain the identity of human culture, which is based on our accumulated knowledge, and to improve the general cultural level of society. According to Stuart Jordan, a retired senior staff scientist at NASA's Goddard Space Flight Center, and currently president of the Institute for Science and Human Values, widespread ignorance and superstition remain "major obstacles to progress to a more humanistic world"[4] in which prosperity, security, justice, good health and access to culture are equally accessible to all humans. He argues that the proliferation of the undesirable consequences of scientific knowledge—such as overpopulation, social inequality, nuclear arms and global climate change—resulted from the abandonment of the key principle of the Enlightenment: the use of reason under a humanistic framework.

When discussing education, we should therefore consider not only those who have no access to basic education, but also a considerable fraction of the populations of developed countries who have no recent science education. The Eurobarometer survey mentioned provides a striking argument: On average, only half of the surveyed Europeans knew that electrons are smaller than atoms, almost a third believed that the Sun goes around the Earth, and nearly a quarter of them affirmed that earliest humans coexisted with dinosaurs. Another type of passive ignorance that is on the increase among the public of industrialised countries, especially among young people, is an indifference to socio-political affairs beyond their own individual and immediate well-being.

Ignorance may have a relevant influence on politics in democracies because ignorant people are more easily manipulated, or because their votes may depend on irrelevant details, such as a candidate's physical appearance or performance in public debates. A democracy should be based on an informed society. Education *sensu lato*—including both formal learning and cultural education—is therefore crucial for developing personal freedom of thought and free will, which will lead to adequate representation and better government.[5]

To improve the cultural level of human societies is a long-term venture in which science will need to play a critical role. We first need to accept that scientific reasoning is intimately linked to human nature: Humanity did not explicitly adopt science as the preferred tool for acquiring knowledge after choosing among a set of possibilities; we simply used our own mental functioning to explain the world. If reason is a universal human feature, any knowledge can be transmitted and understood by everyone without the need for alien constraints, not unlike art or music.

Moreover, science has demonstrated that it is a supreme mechanism to explain the world, to solve problems and to fulfil human needs. A fundamental condition of science is its dynamic nature: the constant revision and re-evaluation of the existing knowledge. Every scientific theory is always under scrutiny and questioned whenever new evidence seems to challenge its validity. No other knowledge system has demonstrated this capacity, and even, the defenders of faith-based systems are common users of medical services and technological facilities that have emerged from scientific knowledge.

For these reasons, formal education from primary school to high school should therefore place a much larger emphasis on teaching young people how science has shaped and advanced human culture and well-being, but also that science flourishes best when scientists are left free to apply human reason to understand the world. This also means that we need to educate the educators and consequently to adopt adequate science curricula at university education departments. Scientists themselves must get more involved both in schools and universities.

But scientists will also have to get more engaged with society in general. The improvement of human culture and society relies on more diffuse structural and functional patterns. In the case of science, its diffusion to the general public is commonly called the popularisation of science and can involve scientists themselves, rather than journalists and other communicators. In this endeavour, scientists should be actively and massively involved. Scientists—especially those working in public institutions—should make a greater effort to communicate to society what science is and what is not; how is it done; what are its main results; and what are they useful for. This would be the best way of demystifying science and scientists and upgrading society's scientific literacy.

In summary, putting a stronger emphasis on formal science education and on raising the general cultural level of society should lead to a more enlightened knowledge-based society—as opposed to the H2020 vision of a knowledge-based economy—that is less susceptible to dogmatic moral systems. Scientists should still use the other arguments—technological progress, improved health and well-being and economic gains—to justify their work, but better education would provide the additional support needed to convince citizens about the usefulness of science beyond its economic value. Science is not only necessary for humanity to thrive socially, environmentally and economically in both the short and the long term, but it is also the best tool available to satisfy the fundamental human thirst for knowledge, as well as to maintain and enhance the human cultural heritage, which is knowledge-based by definition.

Endnotes

1. Japan Science and Technology Agency. 2013. Overview of JST program and organisation 2013–2014. http://www.jst.go.jp/EN/JST_Brochure_2013.pdf. Last accessed: March 20, 2014.

2. McGucken W. On freedom and planning in science: the Society for Freedom in Science, 1940–46. Minerva. 1978;16:42–72.

3. Costanza R, Kubiszewski I, Giovannini E, Lovins H, McGlade J, Pickett KE. Time to leave GDP behind. Nature. 2014;505:283–285.

4. Jordan S. The Enlightenment Vision. Science, Reason and the Promise of a Better Future. Amherst: Promethous Books; 2012.

5. Rull V. Conservation, human values and democracy. EMBO Rep. 2014;15:17–20.

Without Animals, Scientific Medical Research Would Falter

Oxford University

Oxford University is the oldest university in the English-speaking world and continues to be a world leader in education.

Around half the diseases in the world have no treatment. Understanding how the body works and how diseases progress, and finding cures, vaccines or treatments, can take many years of painstaking work using a wide range of research techniques. There is overwhelming scientific consensus worldwide that some research using animals is still essential for medical progress.

Animal research in the UK is strictly regulated. For more details on the regulations governing research using animals, go to the UK regulations page (https://www.ox.ac.uk/news-and-events/animal-research/UK-regulations-on-research-using-animals).

Why Is Animal Research Necessary?

There is overwhelming scientific consensus worldwide that some animals are still needed in order to make medical progress.

Where animals are used in research projects, they are used as part of a range of scientific techniques. These might include human trials, computer modelling, cell culture, statistical techniques, and others. Animals are only used for parts of research where no other techniques can deliver the answer.

A living body is an extraordinarily complex system. You cannot reproduce a beating heart in a test tube or a stroke on a computer. While we know a lot about how a living body works, there is an enormous amount we simply don't know: the interaction between all the different parts of a living system, from molecules to cells to systems like respiration and circulation, is incredibly complex. Even if we knew how every element worked and interacted with every

"Research Using Animals: An Overview," Oxford University. Reprinted by permission.

other element, which we are a long way from understanding, a computer hasn't been invented that has the power to reproduce all of those complex interactions—while clearly you cannot reproduce them all in a test tube.

While humans are used extensively in Oxford research, there are some things which it is ethically unacceptable to use humans for. There are also variables which you can control in a mouse (like diet, housing, clean air, humidity, temperature, and genetic makeup) that you could not control in human subjects.

Is It Morally Right to Use Animals for Research?

Most people believe that in order to achieve medical progress that will save and improve lives, perhaps millions of lives, limited and very strictly regulated animal use is justified. That belief is reflected in the law, which allows for animal research only under specific circumstances, and which sets out strict regulations on the use and care of animals. It is right that this continues to be something society discusses and debates, but there has to be an understanding that without animals we can only make very limited progress against diseases like cancer, heart attack, stroke, diabetes, and HIV.

It's worth noting that animal research benefits animals too: more than half the drugs used by vets were developed originally for human medicine.

Aren't Animals Too Different from Humans to Tell Us Anything Useful?

No. Just by being very complex living, moving organisms they share a huge amount of similarities with humans. Humans and other animals have much more in common than they have differences. Mice share over 90% of their genes with humans. A mouse has the same organs as a human, in the same places, doing the same things. Most of their basic chemistry, cell structure and bodily organisation are the same as ours. Fish and tadpoles share enough characteristics with humans to make them very useful in research. Even flies and worms are used in research extensively and have led to research breakthroughs (though these species are not regulated by the Home Office and are not in the Biomedical Sciences Building).

What Does Research Using Animals Actually Involve?

The sorts of procedures research animals undergo vary, depending on the research. Breeding a genetically modified mouse counts as a procedure and this represents a large proportion of all procedures carried out. So does having an MRI (magnetic resonance image) scan, something which is painless and which humans undergo for health checks. In some circumstances, being trained to go through a maze or being trained at a computer game also counts as a procedure. Taking blood or receiving medication are minor procedures that many species of animal can be trained to do voluntarily for a food reward. Surgery accounts for only a small minority of procedures. All of these are examples of procedures that go on in Oxford's Biomedical Sciences Building.

Why Must Primates Be Used?

Primates account for under half of one per cent (0.5%) of all animals housed in the Biomedical Sciences Building. They are only used where no other species can deliver the research answer, and we continually seek ways to replace primates with lower orders of animal, to reduce numbers used, and to refine their housing conditions and research procedures to maximise welfare.

However, there are elements of research that can only be carried out using primates because their brains are closer to human brains than mice or rats. They are used at Oxford in vital research into brain diseases like Alzheimer's and Parkinson's. Some are used in studies to develop vaccines for HIV and other major infections.

What Is Done to Primates?

The primates at Oxford spend most of their time in their housing. They are housed in groups with access to play areas where they can groom, forage for food, climb and swing.

Primates at Oxford involved in neuroscience studies would typically spend a couple of hours a day doing behavioural work. This is sitting in front of a computer screen doing learning and memory games for food rewards. No suffering is involved and indeed many of the primates appear to find the games stimulating. They come into the transport cage that takes them to the computer room entirely voluntarily.

After some time (a period of months) demonstrating normal learning and memory through the games, a primate would have surgery to remove a very small amount of brain tissue under anaesthetic. A full course of painkillers is given under veterinary guidance in the same way as any human surgical procedure, and the animals are up and about again within hours, and back with their group within a day. The brain damage is minor and unnoticeable in normal behaviour: the animal interacts normally with its group and exhibits the usual natural behaviours. In order to find out about how a disease affects the brain it is not necessary to induce the equivalent of full-blown disease. Indeed, the more specific and minor the brain area affected, the more focussed and valuable the research findings are.

The primate goes back to behavioural testing with the computers and differences in performance, which become apparent through these carefully designed games, are monitored.

At the end of its life the animal is humanely killed and its brain is studied and compared directly with the brains of deceased human patients.

Primates at Oxford involved in vaccine studies would simply have a vaccination and then have monthly blood samples taken.

What's the Difference Between "Total Held" and "On Procedure"?

Primates (macaques) at Oxford would typically spend a couple of hours a day doing behavioural work, sitting in front of a computer screen doing learning and memory games for food rewards. This is non-invasive and done voluntarily for food rewards and does not count as a procedure. After some time (a period of months) demonstrating normal learning and memory through the games, a primate would have surgery under anaesthetic to remove a very small amount of brain tissue. The primate quickly returns to behavioural testing with the computers, and differences in performance, which become apparent through these carefully designed puzzles, are monitored. A primate which has had this surgery is counted as "on procedure." Both stages are essential for research into understanding brain function which is necessary to develop treatments for conditions including Alzheimer's, Parkinson's and schizophrenia.

Why Has the Overall Number Held Gone Down?

Numbers vary year on year depending on the research that is currently undertaken. In general, the University is committed to reducing, replacing and refining animal research.

You Say Primates Account for Under 0.5% of Animals, So That Means You Have at Least 16,000 Animals in the Biomedical Sciences Building in Total—Is That Right?

Numbers change daily so we cannot give a fixed figure, but it is in that order.

Aren't There Alternative Research Methods?

There are very many non-animal research methods, all of which are used at the University of Oxford and many of which were pioneered here. These include research using humans; computer models and simulations; cell cultures and other in vitro work; statistical modelling; and large-scale epidemiology. Every research project which uses animals will also use other research methods in addition. Wherever possible non-animal research methods are used. For many projects, of course, this will mean no animals are needed at all. For others, there will be an element of the research which is essential for medical progress and for which there is no alternative means of getting the relevant information.

How Have Humans Benefited from Research Using Animals?

As the Department of Health states, research on animals has contributed to almost every medical advance of the last century.

Without animal research, medicine as we know it today wouldn't exist. It has enabled us to find treatments for cancer, antibiotics for infections (which were developed in Oxford laboratories), vaccines to prevent some of the most deadly and debilitating viruses, and surgery for injuries, illnesses and deformities.

Life expectancy in this country has increased, on average, by almost three months for every year of the past century. Within the living memory of many people diseases such as polio, turberculosis, leukaemia and diphtheria killed or crippled thousands every year. But now, doctors are able to prevent or treat many more diseases or carry out life-saving operations—all thanks to research which at some stage involved animals.

Each year, millions of people in the UK benefit from treatments that have been developed and tested on animals. Animals have been used for the development of blood transfusions, insulin for diabetes, anaesthetics, anticoagulants, antibiotics, heart and lung machines for open heart surgery, hip replacement surgery, transplantation, high blood pressure medication, replacement heart valves, chemotherapy for leukaemia and life support systems for premature babies. More than 50 million prescriptions are written annually for antibiotics.

We May Have Used Animals in the Past to Develop Medical Treatments, But Are They Really Needed in the 21st Century?

Yes. While we are committed to reducing, replacing and refining animal research as new techniques make it possible to reduce the number of animals needed, there is overwhelming scientific consensus worldwide that some research using animals is still essential for medical progress. It only forms one element of a whole research programme which will use a range of other techniques to find out whatever possible without animals. Animals would be used for a specific element of the research that cannot be conducted in any alternative way.

How Will Humans Benefit in Future?

The development of drugs and medical technologies that help to reduce suffering among humans and animals depends on the carefully regulated use of animals for research. In the 21st century scientists are continuing to work on treatments for cancer, stroke, heart disease, HIV, malaria, tuberculosis, diabetes, neurodegenerative diseases like Alzheimer's and Parkinson's, and very many more diseases that cause suffering and death. Genetically modified mice play a crucial role in future medical progress as understanding of how genes are involved in illness is constantly increasing.

Biological Engineering and Animal Models Support Medical Research

Teal Burrell

Teal Burrell is a science writer with a PhD in neuroscience. Her work has been published widely, including in New Scientist, Discover, *and* NOVA.

Deep in a lab at the Wyss Institute for Biologically Inspired Engineering at Harvard University, Dr. Donald Ingber has reconstructed a human lung. It absorbs oxygen like a normal human lung. It also transmits that oxygen to blood cells flowing beneath. White blood cells flock to foreign bodies that try to infect its tissue, surrounding the invaders and stamping them out. In many ways, it's indistinguishable from the lungs that rise and fall inside you and me, with one exception. This lung is on a microchip.

On these microchips smaller than your thumb, Ingber, director of the Wyss Institute, has reconstructed the complicated interface between lungs and their capillaries. The core of the device is a tiny tube created by microfabrication—a technique used to make structures on the micrometer scale—which is divided in two by a flexible, porous membrane. Human lung cells line the top of the membrane, and capillary cells coat the underside. Air flows through the upper chamber, and a liquid containing human blood cells runs through the lower chamber. Graduate students apply suction to compartments on the sides, mechanically stretching the membrane and its tissue to simulate the rise and fall of our own chest

Ingber's lung-on-a-chip isn't just a breakthrough because it mimics a human organ, but because it does so in more ways than one. The lung cells that line the upper chamber stand in for your lung's alveoli, the microscopic air sacs where gasses pass in and out of the blood stream. As grad students stretch the chamber, it fills with air, passing oxygen through the capillary cells on the other side of the membrane to the blood cells streaming through the lower chamber.

Just as with human lungs, these cells are susceptible to infections. When Ingber's team added bacteria to the airspace of the lung-on-a-chip, white blood cells swarmed to the bacteria. Again, just as they would in a real lung. As Ingber's team pumped the airspace full of various foreign bodies, they discovered something more—that breathing increases the absorption of airborne particulates, like those found in pollution and smog, ten-fold.

They have also tested the toxicity of a cancer drug known to fill patient's lungs with fluid, a condition known as pulmonary edema. When they gave the lung-on-a-chip the same relative dose given to humans over the same timeframe, the drug caused fluid to shift from the blood vessel into the airspace, mimicking a pulmonary edema. The degree to which Ingber's lung-on-a-chip can emulate a real human organ is uncanny. It's all possible because the lung-on-a-chip wasn't designed with just one purpose in mind. It is, Ingber says, "a toxicity model, a drug efficacy model, and a human disease model."

But perhaps their greatest feat will be the replacement of animal models in research studies. Animals such as chimpanzees, mice, and guinea pigs have been used in medical research for centuries, and they have taught us much about anatomy and physiology. But in recent decades, we've realized the limitations of animal models. In some cases, animal organs and systems serve as passable stand-ins for their human equivalents, but in many cases they do not. Ingber's lung-on-a-chip is one of many new attempts at replacing animal models with more effective analogs.

The Animal Problem

The pharmaceutical industry has a problem: about 90% of drug trials fail. Treatments often seem promising when tested in animals, encouraging pharmaceutical companies to start clinical trials that test safety and efficacy in human patients. But the majority of the time, the investment doesn't pay off. Some are pointing their fingers at animal models, saying they don't accurately represent the human disorder they are designed to mimic. Moreover, their response to treatments doesn't predict a human's response and experiments using them often paint an overly optimistic picture.

Ray Greek, president of Americans for Medical Advancement, a group that seeks to restrict the use of animals in medical research, is among those questioning the efficacy of animal models. Often research animals are bred or genetically modified to develop characteristics of a human disease such as diabetes or Alzheimer's disease. While most drugs used to treat those afflictions don't act on genes directly, genes do make proteins that drugs bind to, so tiny differences between species could be the difference between a treatment's success and failure, Greek says. "Really tiny differences can make a gene lethal to you but perfectly fine for a monkey or a chimp or a mouse," he says. "That's Evolution 101. Different genes do different things in different species."

For many diseases, animal models can be challenging to develop. For others, like neurological and neurodegenerative diseases, it's even more difficult. "The time that a mouse lives— which is about two or three years—is about seventy years less than it requires a human to develop some of these disorders," says Dr. Christopher Austin, director of the National Center for Advancing Translational Sciences. Austin says researchers try to manipulate mutations to make their effects even more severe, but "because you have to speed it up to make it happen much faster, you think maybe it's not terribly surprising it would not be predictive."

Besides genetic models, there are a number of different ways researchers simulate diseases in animals, including by introducing an infection or administering a drug. These, too, can be problematic. Take traumatic brain injury, for example. In a controlled experiment, the procedure is standardized such that all mice receive the same injury. On the football field, however, no two injuries may be the same. A neurologically complex disease like schizophrenia is hard to model in an animal in the first place—you can't ask a mouse questions, after all—so testing if a drug reduces symptoms is even more difficult.

Not only are induced diseases and conditions often different in animals, but how we treat them doesn't always translate well to humans. Livers of different species metabolize drugs differently, for example, so toxicity may vary. And in the laboratory, a stroke can be induced and then treated immediately; in real world situations with humans, the time between stroke and treatment is often longer and much more variable.

Austin notes that scientists appreciate these problems. "For all kinds of reasons, scientists would love to have some other way to study most phenomena than using animals," Austin says. "I don't know a single scientist who is not trying to reduce, refine, or replace animal use whenever possible. It's just that for many indications, for many applications, for many diseases—particularly in the neurosciences—there is no alternative. That's the problem."

Possible Replacements

To sidestep the problems with animal models, some scientists use cellular models, which are often derived from human tissues. One way to obtain human cells is to use induced pluripotent stem cells, also known as iPS cells, made from adult tissues such as skin or blood which are reprogrammed into stem cells that can then become any type of cell in the body. This method is useful for studying how a particular drug binds to a receptor, for example, and how the cell responds. But it's not perfect. "What happens to an isolated cell—even a human cell—growing on a dish, on plastic, is likely to be very different from how that cell is going to react in a tissue surrounded by other cells," Austin cautions.

This is where Ingber's organs-on-chips are useful. The chips more closely represent real, live tissue, with various cell types, arranged as in a human, along with their three-dimensional interactions. Importantly, cells grown in a single layer on a dish can't mimic motion, like the simulated breathing of the lung-on-a-chip. Motion is important in other organs, too. Ingber's group has modeled an intestine, predictably called the gut-on-a-chip. In addition to hosting the various cell types that make up an intestinal wall, the gut-on-a-chip also pulses in waves, just like our gastrointestinal tracts do to move food along.

Not only does that motion create a more realistic simulation, it also helps the cells thrive. That's because Ingber's chips don't just host human cells. The gut-on-a-chip also contains some of the same microbes found in a living human's gut. When cells are grown in culture, scientists often try to keep them free of microbes. Any whiff of contamination can kill the other cells. However, in the gut-on-a-chip, fluid flowing through the chamber, along with the peristalsis-like motion, helps gut microbes grow in a healthy, symbiotic way. That allows Ingber's group to study how microbes contribute to health and disease.

By incorporating both lung and capillary cells in a manipulatable structure, the lung-on-a-chip enables more realistic simulations.

Currently, Ingber's group is working on replicating nearly every kind of organ and tissue, including kidneys, livers, and bone marrow. Eventually, he even hopes to connect different organs to make what he calls a human-body-on-a-chip. "Imagine delivering a drug by aerosol to the lung chip, watch it flow over to the liver and see if it's metabolized into different breakdown products—which is what happens in animals and humans—and then see if that's peed out by the kidney." You could test which dose would be optimal to slow the heart, for example, or check if a chemotherapy drug kills bone marrow cells. Ingber notes that is "what we do in animals, effectively, but it would be all human."

Organs-on-chips also could be used to study how genetic variability between people changes how drugs and treatments work. Greek says future treatments need to be based on a person's individual genome, a concept known as pharmacogenetics. "Right now, a drug that cures you of a particular kind of cancer may not cure me," Greek says. "And a drug that I can take for hypertension may work well for me…but you may have a gene that causes a very severe side effect and you won't know until you take the drug." Human clinical trials do test safety and efficacy, but Greek is concerned that they don't capture enough of the variability among people. Because of this, he warns, "everybody who takes a drug is a guinea pig."

Austin speculates that organs-on-chips could be used with pharmacogenetics to address Greek's concern. "It's interesting to think about the potential intersection between organoid tissue chip technology and iPS technology and personalized medicine technology," he says. Austin imagines taking iPS cells from 100 people and putting them on chips, then assessing the variation in responses to drugs. It would be faster, cheaper, and safer than testing in animals or humans. "You could do it very quickly," he says. "You could do it in an afternoon."

Or Do We Refine?

Jonathan Kimmelman, a bioethicist at McGill University, doesn't think we need to do away with animal models entirely, but thinks we can improve them. He believes part of the reason why treatments on animals models don't always translate well to humans is the way preclinical research—including testing on animal models—is designed. Once a treatment makes it to clinical trials, which test safety and efficacy in human subjects, there are many rules and regulations in place to prevent bias. One is blinding, where researchers don't know which treatment the subject received, and another is randomization, where treatment groups are randomly assigned. However, these procedures are only used sporadically in preclinical research, which often involves animals. A recent review of 300 animal studies found that only 14% used blinding and just 13% used randomization.

Another issue is publication bias, where studies with positive results touting the success of a new drug are far more likely to be published than studies with negative results. "That means that when results do get published, you only see a slice or a narrow band of the most positive and encouraging findings," Kimmelman says. "What's missing is perhaps the bottom part of the iceberg, which are inconclusive or negative animal findings."

As decisions are made about clinical trials, this vital information is often missing. For example, in 1980, researchers suspected that lorcainide, an anti-arrhythmic drug, might be a promising treatment following a heart attack. They hypothesized that, since lorcainide decreased abnormal heart rhythms in non-heart attack patients, it would be helpful in for those who suffered from a heart attack, a population more likely to have abnormal heart rhythms. They tested it on a small group of 100 volunteers. Of the 50 people who were treated with lorcainide, ten died. Only one person from the control group given the placebo died. Lorcainide was abandoned as a post-heart attack treatment, but the trial was never published. So when other companies investigated anti-arrhythmic drugs for heart attack patients, they were unaware of lorcainide's failure. In later trials, when the drugs were again given to people following heart attacks, even more people died.

In the years since, safety regulations for clinical trials have increased dramatically. One current requirement is prospective registration, which requires that details of the study—such as the drug to be tested, the expected enrollment, and the definition of success—are recorded in a publicly accessible database before the study starts. Once the study is completed, researchers can search the database and learn the results of the experiment—even if it was not published in a peer-reviewed journal. Kimmelman would like to see the same registration process used in hypothesis-driven animal studies, such as testing the efficacy of a drug, for example.

"There are no registries out there for prospectively stating the design of an experiment," Kimmelman says. "Prospective registries are crucial for preventing publication bias."

The Middle Road

Ingber also acknowledges that although animal models have their flaws, we cannot get rid of them entirely. His organs-on-a-chip and proposed human-on-a-chip offer promising ways to reduce dependence on animal models, but they are not the same thing as a whole, living organism. "There are certain things in animals you are not going to replace on chips, like behavior for example."

"Sometimes people don't realize," Austin says, that animal models "are absolutely essential for what's going on in medical research now. If animals stop being used, progress in medical research would slow dramatically and probably screech to a halt in some cases. Many of the advances that we take for granted now have happened through the use of animal models."

Researchers are increasingly moving away from using animals to model an entire disease, but rather to replicate one aspect that could be treated with a particular drug or intervention. For example, mice bred to be obese and hyperglycemic can be used to study type 2 diabetes. The mice aren't perfect models of type 2 diabetes—they do not have beta cell dysfunction, for instance, which causes insufficient insulin levels in the human disease—but researchers use them to test drugs that improve insulin resistance specifically. "There are many examples of where those particular aspects of a disease or human physiology may actually be reproduced quite faithfully in a particular animal model," Austin says.

Computational advances may also help extend the insight gained from animal models. The European Union's Human Brain Project, which aims to build a brain from supercomputers, is just one example. It's an ambitious project—one that won't be completed for at least a decade. But if it meets its goals, it will hopefully give us a better appreciation for the neurological differences between animals and humans. Eventually, that may lead to better treatments.

"Animal models are not going away," Ingber says. "But we hope, over time, one animal at a time, maybe we can replace—maybe we can show this chip can replace what people were measuring for this particular model. Maybe we can use less animals," he adds. "Everyone knows it's a problem that needs to be solved."

Artificial Intelligence Research and Technology Must Be Carefully Monitored

Kai Kupferschmidt

Kai Kupferschmidt is a contributing writer to Science *magazine. He is based in Berlin, Germany, and specializes in the topics of evolution, nutrition, science policy, food science, and infectious disease.*

Philosopher Nick Bostrom believes it's entirely possible that artificial intelligence (AI) could lead to the extinction of *Homo sapiens*. In his 2014 bestseller *Superintelligence: Paths, Dangers, Strategies*, Bostrom paints a dark scenario in which researchers create a machine capable of steadily improving itself. At some point, it learns to make money from online transactions and begins purchasing goods and services in the real world. Using mail-ordered DNA, it builds simple nanosystems that in turn create more complex systems, giving it ever more power to shape the world.

Now suppose the AI suspects that humans might interfere with its plans, writes Bostrom, who's at the University of Oxford in the United Kingdom. It could decide to build tiny weapons and distribute them around the world covertly. "At a pre-set time, nanofactories producing nerve gas or target-seeking mosquito-like robots might then burgeon forth simultaneously from every square meter of the globe."

For Bostrom and a number of other scientists and philosophers, such scenarios are more than science fiction. They're studying which technological advances pose "existential risks" that could wipe out humanity or at least end civilization as we know it—and what could be done to stop them. "Think of what we're trying to do as providing a scientific red team for the things that could threaten our species," says philosopher Huw Price, who heads the Centre for the Study of Existential Risk (CSER) here at the University of Cambridge.

The idea of science eliminating the human race can be traced all the way back to *Frankenstein*. In Mary Shelley's novel, the monster gets angry at his creator, Victor Frankenstein, for having spurned him. He kills Frankenstein's little brother William, but then offers the doctor a deal: Make a female companion for me and we will leave you in peace and go to South America to live out our days. Frankenstein starts working on the bride, but realizes that the couple might reproduce and outcompete humans: "A race of devils would be propagated upon the earth who might make the very existence of the species of man a condition precarious and full of terror." He destroys the half-finished female, reigniting the creature's wrath and bringing about his own demise.

"I think *Frankenstein* illustrates the point beautifully," says physicist Max Tegmark of the Massachusetts Institute of Technology (MIT) in Cambridge, a board member of CSER and a co-founder of a similar think tank, the Future of Life Institute (FLI), near MIT. "We humans gradually develop ever-more-powerful technology, and the more powerful the tech becomes, the more careful we have to be, so we don't screw up with it."

The study of existential risks is still a tiny field, with at most a few dozen people at three centers. Not everyone is convinced it's a serious academic discipline. Most civilization-ending scenarios—which include humanmade pathogens, armies of nanobots, or even the idea that our world is a simulation that might be switched off—are wildly unlikely, says Joyce Tait, who studies regulatory issues in the life sciences at the Innogen Institute in Edinburgh. The only true existential threat, she says, is a familiar one: a global nuclear war. Otherwise, "There is nothing on the horizon."

Harvard University psychologist Steven Pinker calls existential risks a "useless category" and warns that "Frankensteinian fantasies" could distract from real, solvable threats such as climate change and nuclear war. "Sowing fear about hypothetical disasters, far from safeguarding the future of humanity, can endanger it," he writes in his upcoming book *Enlightenment Now: The Case for Reason, Science, Humanism, and Progress.*

But advocates predict the field will only get more important as scientific and technological progress accelerates. As Bostrom pointed out in one paper, much more research has been done on dung beetles or *Star Trek* than on the risks of human extinction. "There is a very good case for saying that science has basically ignored" the issue, Price says.

Humanity has always faced the possibility of an untimely end. Another asteroid of the size that ended the dinosaurs' reign could hit Earth; a volcanic cataclysm could darken the skies for years and starve us all.

But existential risks arising from scientific advances were literally fiction until 16 July 1945, when the first atomic bomb was detonated. Based on some back-of-the-envelope calculations, physicist Edward Teller had concluded that the explosion might set off a global chain reaction, "igniting" the atmosphere. "Although we now know that such an outcome was physically impossible, it qualifies as an existential risk that was present at the time," Bostrom writes. Within 2 decades a real existential risk emerged, from growing stockpiles of the new weapons. Physicists had finally assembled Frankenstein's bride.

Other scientific disciplines may soon pose similar threats. "In this century we will introduce entirely new kinds of phenomena, give ourselves new kinds of powers to reshape the world," Bostrom says. Biotechnology is cheaper and easier to handle than nuclear technology has ever been. Nanotechnology is making rapid strides. And at a 2011 meeting in Copenhagen, Estonian computer programmer and Skype co-developer Jaan Tallinn told Price about his deep fears about AI during a shared taxi ride. "I'd never met anyone at that point who took that as seriously as Jaan," says Price, who was about to start working at the University of Cambridge.

Price introduced Tallinn to astronomer Martin Rees, a former president of the Royal Society, who had long warned that as science progresses, it will increasingly place the power to destroy civilization in the hands of individuals. The trio decided to launch CSER, the second such center after Bostrom's Future of Humanity Institute in Oxford, which he launched in 2005. CSER's name was "a deliberate attempt to push the idea of existential risk more towards the mainstream," Price says. "We were aware that people think of these issues as a little bit flaky."

CSER has recruited some big-name supporters: The scientific advisory board includes physicist Stephen Hawking, Harvard biologist George Church, global health leader Peter Piot, and tech entrepreneur Elon Musk. In a sign of just how small the field still is, Tallinn also co-founded FLI in 2014, and Church, Musk, Hawking, Bostrom, and Rees all serve on its scientific advisory board. (Actor Morgan Freeman, who has literally played God, is also an FLI adviser.)

Most of CSER's money comes from foundations and individuals, including Tallinn, who donated about $8 million to existential risk researchers in 2017. CSER's academic output has been "ephemeral" so far, Tallinn concedes. But the center was set up as "a sort of training ground for existential risk research," he says, with academics from elsewhere coming to visit and then "infecting" their own institutions with ideas.

The dozen people working at CSER itself—little more than a large room in an out-of-the-way building near the university's occupational health service—organize talks, convene scientists to discuss future developments, and publish on topics from regulation of synthetic biology to ecological tipping points. A lot of their time is spent pondering end-of-the-world scenarios and potential safeguards.

Church says a "crunch," in which a large part of the world population dies, is more likely than a complete wipe-out. "You don't have to turn the entire planet into atoms," he says. Disrupting electrical grids and other services on a huge scale or releasing a deadly pathogen could create chaos, topple governments, and send humanity into a downward spiral. "You end up with a medieval level of culture," Church says. "To me that is the end of humanity."

Existential risks stemming from the life sciences are perhaps easiest to imagine. Pathogens have proved capable of killing off entire species, such as the frogs that have fallen victim to the amphibian fungus *Batrachochytrium dendrobatidis*. And four influenza pandemics have swept the world in the past century, including one that killed up to 50 million people in 1918 and 1919. Researchers are already engineering pathogens that in principle could be even more dangerous. Worries about studies that made the H5N1 bird flu strain more easily transmissible between mammals led the United States to halt such research until late last year. Terrorists or rogue states could use labmade agents as a weapon, or an engineered plague could be released accidentally.

Rees has publicly wagered that by 2020, "bioterror or bioerror will lead to 1 million casualties in a single event." Harvard microbiologist Marc Lipsitch has calculated that the likelihood of a labmade flu virus leading to an accidental pandemic is between one in 1000 and one in 10,000 per year of research in one laboratory; Ron Fouchier of Erasmus MC in Rotterdam, the Netherlands, one of the researchers involved in the H5N1 studies, has dismissed that estimate, saying the real risk is more like one in 33 billion per year and lab.

One measure against "bioerror" might be to make researchers who carry out risky experiments buy insurance; that would require an independent assessment of the risk and would force researchers to face up to it, Lipsitch says. Still, the most important countermeasure is to strengthen the world's capacity to contain an outbreak early on, he adds, for instance with vaccines. "For biological risks, short of a really massive, coordinated, parallel attack around the world, the only way we are going to get to a really catastrophic scenario is by failing to control a smaller scenario," he says.

Viruses are unlikely to kill every last human, Bostrom says; for him and others, it is AI that poses truly existential threats.

Most scenarios center on machines out-smarting humans, a feat called "super-intelligence." If such AI were ever achieved and it acquired a will of its own, it might turn malevolent and actively seek to destroy humans, like HAL, the computer that goes rogue aboard a spaceship in Stanley Kubrick's film *2001: A Space Odyssey.*

Most AI experts worry less about machines rising up to overthrow their creators, however, than about them making a fatal mistake. To Tallinn, the most plausible way in which AI could end humanity is if it simply pursued its goals and, along the way, heedlessly created an environment fatal to humans. "Imagine a situation where the temperature rises by 100° or is lowered by 100°. We'd go extinct in a matter of minutes," Tallinn says. Tegmark agrees: "The real problem with AI is not malice, it's incompetence," he says.

A current-day analogy is the 2015 tragedy in which a suicidal Germanwings pilot told his plane's computer to descend to an altitude of 100 meters while flying over the French Alps. The machine complied, killing all 150 on board, even though it had GPS and a topographic map. "It did not have a clue about even the simplest human goal," Tegmark says. To avoid such calamities, scientists are trying to figure out how to teach AI human values and make sure they stick, a problem called "value alignment." "There might be fewer than 20 people who work full time on technical AI safety research," Bostrom says. "A few more talented people might substantially increase the rate of progress."

Critics say these efforts are unlikely to be useful, because future threats are inherently unpredictable. Predictions were a problem in every "foresight exercise" Tait has taken part in, she says. "We're just not good at it." Even if you foresee a risk, economic, political, and societal circumstances will all affect how it plays out. "Unless you know not only what is going to happen, but how it is going to happen, the information is not much use in terms of doing something about it," Tait says.

Pinker thinks the scenarios reveal more about human obsessions than real risks. We are drawn to prospects "that are highly improbable while having big impacts on our fitness, such as illicit sex, violent death, and Walter-Mittyish feats of glory," he writes. "Apocalyptic storylines are undoubtedly gripping—they are a supernormal stimulus for our morbid obsessions." Sure, he says, one can imagine a malevolent, powerful AI that people can no longer control. "The way to deal with this threat is straightforward: Don't build one."

Tallinn argues it's better to be safe than sorry. A 2017 survey showed that 34% of AI experts believed the risks associated with their work are an important problem; 5% said they are "one of the most important problems." "Imagine you're on a plane, and 40% of experts think that there is a bomb on this plane," Tallinn says. "You're not going to wait for the remaining experts to be convinced."

Price says that critics who accuse him and his colleagues of indulging in science fiction are not entirely wrong: Producing doomsday scenarios is not that different from what Shelley did. "The first step is to imagine that range of possibilities, and at that point, the kind of imagination that is used in science fiction and other forms of literature and film is likely to be extremely important," he says.

Scientists have an obligation to be involved, says Tegmark, because the risks are unlike any the world has faced before. Every time new technologies emerged in the past, he points out, humanity waited until their risks were apparent before learning to curtail them. Fire killed people and destroyed cities, so humans invented fire extinguishers and flame retardants. With automobiles came traffic deaths—and then seat belts and airbags. "Humanity's strategy is to learn from mistakes," Tegmark says. "When the end of the world is at stake, that is a terrible strategy."

It Is Right to Question Medical Experiments That Use Humans

Anthony Wrigley

Anthony Wrigley is a senior lecturer in ethics at Keele University in the United Kingdom.

In January 1944, a 17-year-old Navy seaman named Nathan Schnurman volunteered to test protective clothing for the Navy. Following orders, he donned a gas mask and special clothes and was escorted into a 10-foot by 10-foot chamber, which was then locked from the outside. Sulfur mustard and Lewisite, poisonous gasses used in chemical weapons, were released into the chamber and, for one hour each day for five days, the seaman sat in this noxious vapor. On the final day, he became nauseous, his eyes and throat began to burn, and he asked twice to leave the chamber. Both times he was told he needed to remain until the experiment was complete. Ultimately Schnurman collapsed into unconsciousness and went into cardiac arrest. When he awoke, he had painful blisters on most of his body. He was not given any medical treatment and was ordered to never speak about what he experienced under the threat of being tried for treason. For 49 years these experiments were unknown to the public.

The Scandal Unfolds

In 1993, the National Academy of Sciences exposed a series of chemical weapons experiments stretching from 1944 to 1975 which involved 60,000 American GIs. At least 4,000 were used in gas-chamber experiments such as the one described above. In addition, more than 210,000 civilians and GIs were subjected to hundreds of radiation tests from 1945 through 1962.

"Human Experimentation: An Introduction to the Ethical Issues," by Anthony Wrigley, Physicians Committee for Responsible Medicine, June 8, 2015. Reprinted by permission.

Testimony delivered to Congress detailed the studies, explaining that "these tests and experiments often involved hazardous substances such as radiation, blister and nerve agents, biological agents, and lysergic acid diethylamide (LSD)....Although some participants suffered immediate acute injuries, and some died, in other cases adverse health problems were not discovered until many years later—often 20 to 30 years or longer."[1]

These examples and others like them—such as the infamous Tuskegee syphilis experiments (1932-72) and the continued testing of unnecessary (and frequently risky) pharmaceuticals on human volunteers—demonstrate the danger in assuming that adequate measures are in place to ensure ethical behavior in research.

Tuskegee Studies

In 1932, the US Public Health Service in conjunction with the Tuskegee Institute began the now notorious "Tuskegee Study of Untreated Syphilis in the Negro Male." The study purported to learn more about the treatment of syphilis and to justify treatment programs for African Americans. Six hundred African American men, 399 of whom had syphilis, became participants. They were given free medical exams, free meals, and burial insurance as recompense for their participation and were told they would be treated for "bad blood," a term in use at the time referring to a number of ailments including syphilis, when, in fact, they did not receive proper treatment and were not informed that the study aimed to document the progression of syphilis without treatment. Penicillin was considered the standard treatment by 1947, but this treatment was never offered to the men. Indeed, the researchers took steps to ensure that participants would not receive proper treatment in order to advance the objectives of the study. Although, the study was originally projected to last only 6 months, it continued for 40 years.

Following a front-page *New York Times* article denouncing the studies in 1972, the Assistant Secretary for Health and Scientific Affairs appointed a committee to investigate the experiment. The committee found the study ethically unjustified and within a month it was ended. The following year, the National Association for the Advancement of Colored People won a $9 million class action suit on behalf of the Tuskegee participants. However, it was not until May 16, 1997, when President Clinton addressed the eight surviving Tuskegee participants and others active in keeping the memory of Tuskegee alive, that a formal apology was issued by the government.

While Tuskegee and the discussed US military experiments stand out in their disregard for the well-being of human subjects, more recent questionable research is usually devoid of obvious malevolent intentions. However, when curiosity is not curbed with compassion, the results can be tragic.

Unnecessary Drugs Mean Unnecessary Experiments

A widespread ethical problem, although one that has not yet received much attention, is raised by the development of new pharmaceuticals. All new drugs are tested on human volunteers. There is, of course, no way subjects can be fully apprised of the risks in advance, as that is what the tests purport to determine. This situation is generally considered acceptable, provided volunteers give "informed" consent. Many of the drugs under development today, however, offer little clinical benefit beyond those available from existing treatments. Many are developed simply to create a patentable variation on an existing drug. It is easy to justify asking informed, consenting individuals to risk limited harm in order to develop new drug therapies for a condition from which they are suffering or for which existing treatments are inadequate. The same may not apply when the drug being tested offers no new benefits to the subjects because they are healthy volunteers, or when the drug offers no significant benefits to anyone because it is essentially a copy of an existing drug.

Manufacturers, of course, hope that animal tests will give an indication of how a given drug will affect humans. However, a full 70 to 75 percent of drugs approved by the Food and Drug

Administration for clinical trials based on promising results in animal tests, ultimately prove unsafe or ineffective for humans.[2] Even limited clinical trials cannot reveal the full range of drug risks. A US General Accounting Office (GAO) study reports that of the 198 new drugs which entered the market between 1976 and 1985, 102 (52 percent) caused adverse reactions that premarket tests failed to predict.[3] Even in the brief period between January and August 1997, at least 53 drugs currently on the market were relabeled due to unexpected adverse effects.[4]

In the GAO study, no fewer than eight of the drugs in question were benzodiazepines, similar to Valium, Librium, and numerous other sedatives of this class. Two were heterocyclic antidepressants, adding little or nothing to the numerous existing drugs of this type. Several others were variations of cephalosporin antibiotics, antihypertensives, and fertility drugs. These are not needed drugs. The risks taken to develop these drugs by trial participants, and to a certain extent by consumers, were not in the name of science, but in the name of market share.

As physicians, we necessarily have a relationship with the pharmaceutical companies that produce, develop, and market drugs involved in medical treatment. A reflective, perhaps critical posture towards some of the standard practices of these companies—such as the routine development of unnecessary drugs—may help to ensure higher ethical standards in research.

Unnecessary Experimentation on Children

Unnecessary and questionable human experimentation is not limited to pharmaceutical development. In experiments at the National Institutes of Health (NIH), a genetically engineered human growth hormone (hGH) is injected into healthy short children. Consent is obtained from parents and affirmed by the children themselves. The children receive 156 injections each year in the hope of becoming taller.

Growth hormone is clearly indicated for hormone-deficient children who would otherwise remain extremely short. Until the early 1980s, they were the only ones eligible to receive it; because it was harvested from human cadavers, supplies were limited. But genetic engineering changed that, and the hormone can now be manufactured in mass quantities. This has led pharmaceutical houses to eye a huge potential market: healthy children who are simply shorter than average. Short stature, of course, is not a disease. The problems short children face relate only to how others react to their height and their own feelings about it. The hGH injection, on the other hand, poses significant risks, both physical and psychological.

These injections are linked in some studies to a potential for increased cancer risk,[5-8] are painful, and may aggravate, rather than reduce, the stigma of short stature.[9,10] Moreover, while growth rate is increased in the short term, it is unclear that the final net height of the child is significantly increased by the treatment.

The Physicians Committee for Responsible Medicine worked to halt these experiments and recommended that the biological and psychological effects of hGH treatment be studied in hormone-deficient children who already receive hGH, and that non-pharmacologic interventions to counteract the stigma of short stature also be investigated. Unfortunately, the hGH studies have continued without modification, putting healthy short children at risk.

Use of Placebo in Clinical Research

Whooping cough, also known as pertussis, is a serious threat to infants, with dangerous and sometimes fatal complications. Vaccination has nearly wiped out pertussis in the US. Uncertainties remain, however, over the relative merits and safety of traditional whole-cell vaccines versus newer, acellular versions, prompting the NIH to propose an experiment testing various vaccines on children.

The controversial part of the 1993 experiment was the inclusion of a placebo group of more than 500 infants who get no protection at all, an estimated 5 percent of whom were expected to develop whooping cough, compared to the 1.4 percent estimated risk for the study group as a whole. Because of these risks, this study would not be permissible in the US. The NIH, however, insisted on the inclusion of a placebo control and therefore initiated the study in Italy where there are fewer restrictions on human research trials. Originally, Italian health officials recoiled from these studies on ethical as well as practical grounds, but persistent pressure from the NIH ensured that the study was conducted with the placebo group.

The use of double-blind placebo-controlled studies is the "gold standard" in the research community, usually for good reason. However, when a well-accepted treatment is available, the use of a placebo control group is not always acceptable and is sometimes unethical.[11] In such cases, it is often appropriate to conduct research using the standard treatment as an active control. The pertussis experiments on Italian children were an example of dogmatic adherence to a research protocol which trumped ethical concerns.

Placebos, Ethics, and Poorer Nations

The ethical problems that placebo-controlled trials raise are especially complicated in research conducted in economically disadvantaged countries. Recently, attention has been brought to studies conducted in Africa on preventing the transmission of HIV from mothers to newborns. Standard treatment for HIV-infected pregnant women in the US is a costly regimen of AZT. This treatment can save the life of one in seven infants born to women with AIDS.[12] Sadly, the cost of AZT treatment is well beyond the means of most of the world's population. This troubling situation has motivated studies to find a cost-effective treatment that can confer at least some benefit in poorer countries where the current standard of care is no treatment at all. A variety of these studies is now underway in which a control group of HIV-positive pregnant women receives no antiretroviral treatment.

Such studies would clearly be unethical in the US where AZT treatment is the standard of care for all HIV-positive mothers. Peter Lurie, M.D., M.P.H., and Sidney Wolfe, M.D., in an editorial in the *New England Journal of Medicine*, hold that such use of placebo controls in research trials in poor nations is unethical as well. They contend that, by using placebo control groups, researchers adopt a double standard leading to "an incentive to use as research subjects those with the least access to health care."[13] Lurie and Wolfe argue that an active control receiving the standard regimen of AZT can and should be compared with promising alternative therapies (such as a reduced dosage of AZT) to develop an effective, affordable treatment for poor countries.

Control Groups and Nutrition

Similar ethical problems are also emerging in nutrition research. In the past, it was ethical for prevention trials in heart disease or other serious conditions to include a control group which received weak nutritional guidelines or no dietary intervention at all. However, that was before diet and lifestyle changes—particularly those using very low fat, vegetarian diets—were shown to reverse existing heart disease, push adult-onset diabetes into remission, significantly lower blood pressure, and reduce the risk of some forms of cancer. Perhaps in the not-too-distant future, such comparison groups will no longer be permissible.

The Ethical Landscape

Ethical issues in human research generally arise in relation to population groups that are vulnerable to abuse. For example, much of the ethically dubious research conducted in poor countries would not occur were the level of medical care not so limited. Similarly, the cruelty of the Tuskegee experiments clearly reflected racial prejudice. The NIH experiments on short children were motivated to counter a fundamentally social problem, the stigma of short stature, with a profitable pharmacologic solution. The unethical military experiments during the Cold War would have been impossible if GIs had had the right to abort assignments or raise complaints. As we address the ethical issues of human experimentation, we often find ourselves traversing complex ethical terrain. Vigilance is most essential when vulnerable populations are involved.

References

1. Frank C. Conahan of the National Security and International Affairs Division of the General Accounting Office, reporting to the Subcommittee of the House Committee on Government Operations.

2. Flieger K. Testing drugs in people. US Food and Drug Administration. September 10, 1997.

3. US General Accounting Office. FDA Drug Review: Postapproval Risks 1976-85. US General Accounting Office, Washington, D.C., 1990.

4. MedWatch, US Food and Drug Administration. Labeling changes related to drug safety. US Food and Drug Administration Home Page; http://www.fda.gov /medwatch/safety.htm. September 10, 1997.

5. Arteaga CL, Osborne CK. Growth inhibition of human breast cancer cells in vitro with an antibody against the type I somatomedin receptor. Cancer Res. 1989;49:6237-6241.

6. Pollak M, Costantino J, Polychronakos C, et al. Effect of tamoxifen on serum insulin-like growth factor I levels in stage I breast cancer patients. J Natl Cancer Inst. 1990;82:1693-1697.

7. Stoll BA. Growth hormone and breast cancer. Clin Oncol. 1992;4:4-5.

8. Stoll BA. Does extra height justify a higher risk of breast cancer? Ann Oncol. 1992;3:29-30.

9. Kusalic M, Fortin C. Growth hormone treatment in hypopituitary dwarfs: longitudinal psychological effects. Canad Psychiatric Asso J. 1975;20:325-331.

10. Grew RS, Stabler B, Williams RW, Underwood LE. Facilitating patient understanding in the treatment of growth delay. Clin Pediatr. 1983;22:685-90.

11. For a more extensive discussion of the ethical status of placebo-controlled trials see especially: Freedman B, Glass KC, Weijer C. Placebo orthodoxy in clinical research II: ethical, legal and regulatory myths. J Law Med Ethics. 1996;24:252-259.

12. Lurie P, Wolfe SM. Unethical trials of interventions to reduce perinatal transmission of the human immunodeficiency virus in developing countries. N Engl J Med. 1997:337:12:853.

13. Ibid, 855.

Unethical Experiments Should Be Prevented, No Matter How Scientifically Valuable

Condé Nast

Condé Nast is a global media company with headquarters in New York and London.

When scientists violate moral taboos, we expect horrific consequences. It's a trope in our storytelling that goes back at least to Mary Shelley's *Frankenstein:* However well-intentioned our fictional scientists may be, their disregard for ethical boundaries will produce not a peer-reviewed paper in *Science* but rather a new race of subhuman killers, a sucking wormhole in space-time, or a profusion of malevolent goo.

In the real world, though, matters aren't so simple. Most scientists will assure you that ethical rules never hinder good research—that there's always a virtuous path to testing any important hypothesis. But ask them in private, perhaps after a drink or three, and they'll confess that the dark side does have its appeal. Bend the rules and some of our deepest scientific conundrums could be elucidated or even resolved: nature versus nurture, the causes of mental illness, even the mystery of how humans evolved from monkeys. These discoveries are just sitting out there, waiting for us to find them, if only we were willing to lose our souls.

What follows are seven creepy experiments—thought experiments, really—that show how contemporary science might advance if it were to toss away the moral compass that guides it. Don't try these at home—or anywhere, for that matter. But also don't pretend you wouldn't like to learn the secrets that these experiments would reveal.

"Seven Creepy Experiments That Could Teach Us So Much (If They Weren't So Wrong)," Condé Nast, July 15, 2011. Reprinted by permission.

Separating Twins

The Experiment: Split up twins after birth—and then control every aspect of their environments.

The premise: In the quest to tease out the interplay of nature and nurture, researchers have one obvious resource: identical twins, two people whose genes are nearly 100 percent the same. But twins almost always grow up together, in essentially the same environment. A few studies have been able to track twins separated at a young age, usually by adoption. But it's impossible to control retroactively for all the ways that the lives of even separated twins are still related. If scientists could control the siblings from the start, they could construct a rigorously designed study. It would be one of the least ethical studies imaginable, but it might be the only way (short of cloning humans for research, which is arguably even less ethical) that we'd ever solve some big questions about genetics and upbringing.

How it works: Expectant mothers of twins would need to be recruited ahead of time so the environments of each sibling could differ from the moment of birth. After choosing what factors to investigate, researchers could construct test homes for the children, ensuring that every aspect of their upbringing, from diet to climate, was controlled and measured.

The payoff: Several disciplines would benefit enormously, but none more than psychology, in which the role of upbringing has long been particularly hazy. Developmental psychologists could arrive at some unprecedented insights into personality—finally explaining, for example, why twins raised together can turn out completely different, while those raised apart can wind up very alike. —Erin Biba

Brain Sampling

The Experiment: Remove brain cells from a live subject to analyze which genes are switched on and which are off.

The premise: You might donate blood or hair for scientific research, but how about a tiny slice of your brain—while you're still alive? Medical ethics wouldn't let you consent to that even if you wanted to, and for good reason: It's an invasive surgery with serious risks. But if enough healthy patients agreed, it could help answer a huge question: How does nurture affect nature, and vice versa? Although scientists recognize in principle that our environment can alter our DNA, they have few documented examples of how these so-called epigenetic changes happen and with what consequences.

Animal studies suggest the consequences could be profound. A 2004 McGill University study of lab rats found that certain maternal behaviors can silence a gene in the hippocampi of their pups, leaving them less able to handle stress hormones. In 2009, a McGill-led team got a hint of a similar effect in humans: In the brains of dead people who had been abused as children and then committed suicide, the analogous gene was largely inhibited. But what about in living brains? When does the shift happen? With brain sampling, we might come to understand the real neurologic toll of child abuse and potentially a great deal more than that.

How it works: Researchers would obtain brain cells just as a surgeon does when conducting a biopsy: After lightly sedating the patient, they would attach a head ring with four pins, using local anesthetic to numb the skin. A surgeon would make an incision a few millimeters wide in the scalp, drill a small hole through the skull, and insert a biopsy needle to grab a tiny bit of tissue. A thin slice would be sufficient, since you need only a few micrograms of DNA. Assuming no infection or surgical error, damage to the brain would be minimal.

The payoff: Such an experiment might answer some deep questions about how we learn. Does reading turn on genes in the prefrontal cortex, the site of higher-order cognition? Does spending lots of time at a batting cage alter the epigenetic status of genes in the motor cortex? Does watching *Real Housewives* alter genes in whatever brain you have left? By correlating experiences with the DNA in our heads, we could better understand how the lives we lead wind up tinkering with the genes we inherited. — Sharon Begley

Embryo Mapping

The Experiment: Insert a tracking agent into a human embryo to monitor its development.

The premise: These days, expectant mothers undergo elaborate tests to make sure their fetus is normal. So, would any of them allow scientists to exploit their future offspring as a science project? Not likely. But without that sort of radical experimentation, we may never fully understand the great remaining mystery of human development: how a tiny clump of cells transforms into a fully formed human being. Today, researchers have the tools to answer that question in principle, thanks to new technology that allows for the tracking of cells' genetic activity over time. If ethics weren't an issue, all they would need was a willing subject—a mother who would let them use her embryo as a guinea pig.

How it works: To trace the activity of different genes within an embryonic cell, researchers could use a synthetic virus to insert a "reporter" gene (green fluorescent protein, for example) that was visually detectable. As that cell divided and differentiated, researchers could actually observe how genes turned on and off at various points in development. This would let them see which developmental switches transform embryonic stem cells into hundreds of types of specialized adult cells—lung, liver, heart, brain, and so on.

The payoff: A fully mapped embryo would give us, for the first time, a front-row seat for the making of a human being. That information could help us direct the evolution of stem cells to repair cellular damage and treat disease (say, by inserting a healthy pool of neurons into the brain of a patient with Parkinson's disease). Comparing the details of human embryonic development to that of other species—similar mapping has already been done on mice, for example—might also reveal the differences in genetic expression that contribute to complex human attributes such as language. But the risks of human embryo mapping are too great to even consider performing it. Not only would the mapping process risk terminating the pregnancy, the viral vector used to insert the reporter gene might disrupt the embryo's DNA and lead, ironically, to developmental defects. —Jennifer Kahn

Optogenetics

The Experiment: Use beams of light to control the activity of brain cells in conscious human beings.

The premise: May I cut open your skull and implant some electronic gizmos in there? Before you say no, listen to what science might get out of the deal. The brain is a nearly infinite knot of electrical connections, and figuring out the purpose of any given circuit is a massive challenge. Much of what we do know comes from studying brain injuries, which let us crudely infer the function of various areas based on the apparent effects of the wounds. Conventional genetic approaches, in which particular genes are chemically disabled or mutated, are more precise—but those techniques take hours or even days to influence the activity of cells, making it hard to trace the impact on mental processes. To really map the brain, scientists will need a tool that is precise but also fast.

How it works: Optogenetics is an experimental method being used with great success in mice. Researchers have engineered a benign virus that, when injected into the brain, makes the ion channels—the switches that turn cells on and off—responsive to light. By flashing focused beams into brain tissue (usually with hair-width fiber-optic strands), researchers can selectively increase or decrease the firing rate of these cells and watch how subjects are affected. Unlike conventional genetic approaches, optogenetic flashes alter neural firing within milliseconds. And by aiming at specific circuits in the brain, it's possible to test theories with great precision.

The payoff: One human brain, when decked out for optogenetic research, would yield unparalleled insight into the workings of the mind. Just imagine if we could silence a few cells in the right prefrontal cortex and make self-awareness disappear. Or if shining a light in the visual cortex prevented us from recognizing the face of a loved one. Ideally, the effects would be only temporary: Once the light was turned off, those deficits would disappear. Such experiments would give us our first detailed understanding of causality in the cortex, revealing how 100 billion neurons work together to endow us with all the impressive talents we take for granted. —Jonah Lehrer

Womb Swapping

The Experiment: Switch the embryos of obese women with those of thin women.

The premise: In vitro fertilization is an expensive and risky procedure as it is. So it's hard to imagine that any mother in an IVF program would ever be willing to swap embryos, entrusting her progeny to another womb while gestating someone else's child herself. But such an act of scientific selflessness could spawn some truly significant breakthroughs. Why? For all that we don't understand about epigenetics—the way that our genes are altered by our environment—the trickiest problem is this: Many of the most important epigenetic influences happen while we're in the womb.

A classic example is obesity. Studies have shown that obese women tend to have overweight children, even before dietary factors kick in. Trouble is, nobody knows how much of that is a product of genes—innate, inherited variations—or epigenetics.

How it works: The experiment would be the same as regular in vitro fertilization, except the fertilized egg of an obese mother would be transferred to the womb of a skinny mother, and vice versa.

The payoff: We would know with much more certainty whether the roots of obesity were primarily genetic or epigenetic—and similar studies could probe other traits. For example, a Canadian team is currently undertaking a massive study, the Maternal-Infant Research on Environmental Chemicals, to isolate the effects of in utero exposure to toxins on a child's genes. With embryo swaps at scientists' disposal, that task wouldn't require statistical guesswork. The answer would be clear as day—even if the ethics were profoundly murky. —Jennifer Kahn

Toxic Heroes

The Experiment: Test each new chemical on a wide range of human volunteers before it comes on the market.

The premise: Under current US regulations, we're all de facto test subjects for a whole range of potential toxins. So why not recruit volunteers to try out chemicals for us? Even with informed consent, medical ethicists would recoil at that idea. But it would almost certainly save lives over time.

To comply with the US Toxic Substances Control Act, manufacturers turn to testing labs, which expose animals—usually rodents—to high levels of the chemical in question. But just because a mouse survives a test doesn't mean that humans will. The only studies we can perform on people are observational: tracking the incidence of adverse effects in those we know to have been exposed. But these studies are fraught with problems. When researchers can find high levels of exposure—for example, workers in factories that make or use the chemical—the number of subjects is often too small to yield reliable results. And with broader-based studies, it becomes extremely difficult to tease out one chemical's effect, since we're all exposed to so many toxins every day.

How it works: Perform all the standard safety tests required by the Toxic Substances Control Act on humans instead of animals. To do so, we'd need to recruit volunteers of varying races and health levels—ideally hundreds for each substance.

The payoff: Toxicology is currently a guessing game. Just think of the controversy over bisphenol A, about which the studies of effects in humans are maddeningly inconclusive. Testing chemicals extensively on groups of people would provide a much more accurate picture of how a given chemical affected us—data that would inform regulators and be shared with the public to help people make their own decisions. An ancillary victory: no more conflicting news reports about what is and isn't good for you.
—Erin Biba

Ape Man

The Experiment: Cross-breed a human with a chimpanzee.

The premise: The great biologist Stephen Jay Gould called it "the most potentially interesting and ethically unacceptable experiment I can imagine." The idea? Mating a human with a chimp. His interest in this monstrosity grew out of his work with snails, closely related species of which can display wide variation in shell architecture. Gould attributed this diversity to a few master genes, which turn on and off the shared genes responsible for constructing the shells. Perhaps, he speculated, the large visible differences between humans and apes were also a factor of developmental timing. He pointed out that adult humans have physical traits, such as larger craniums and wide-set eyes, that resemble infant chimpanzees, a phenomenon known as neoteny—the retention of juvenile traits in adults. Gould theorized that over the course of evolution, a tendency toward neoteny might have helped give rise to human beings. By watching the development of a half-human, half-chimp, researchers could explore this theory in a firsthand (and truly creepy) way.

How it works: It would probably be frighteningly easy: The same techniques used for in vitro fertilization would likely yield a viable hybrid human-chimp embryo. (Researchers have already spanned a comparable genetic gap in breeding a rhesus monkey with a baboon.) Chimps have 24 pairs of chromosomes, and humans 23, but this is not an absolute barrier to breeding. The offspring would likely have an odd number of chromosomes, though, which might make them unable to reproduce themselves. As for the gestation and birth, it could be done the natural way. Chimpanzees are born slightly smaller than humans, on average— around 4 pounds—and so comparative anatomy would argue for growing the embryo in a human uterus.

The payoff: Gould's idea about neoteny remains controversial, to say the least. "It got a lot of scrutiny and has been disproved in many ways," says Daniel Lieberman, a Harvard professor of human evolutionary biology. But Alexander Harcourt, professor emeritus of anthropology at UC Davis, regards neoteny as "still a viable concept." This forbidden experiment would help to resolve that debate and, in a broader sense, illuminate how two species with such similar genomes could be so different. Its outcome would take biologists deep into the origin of the species we care about most: ourselves. Let's just hope we can find a less disturbing route to get there. —Jerry Adler

CHAPTER 3

Should Attacks on Science Be Prevented?

Overview: Is It a Real Scientific Debate?

Dr. Dave Hone

Dr. Dave Hone is a lecturer at Queen Mary College at the University of London. He specializes in dinosaurs and pterosaurs.

One thing that seems to crop up regularly in both bad science journalism and in pseudoscience and non-science is the idea of a scientific debate. We see creationists talking about "teaching both sides" or the idea that there is "a debate over evolution," but there's also more than enough reports in the media with statements like "this study has reignited a debate" to make it a more general pattern. The implication in each case is that there is a genuine split in the scientific community over the relevant issue, and that perhaps one might go to a conference and see a room full of researchers split down the middle with a good number on each side of the divide advocating their position. By extension, if unspoken, this also rather implies that there is a major stack of evidence for each position, if not, surely there would be no split? After all, if all or the vast majority of the data and analyses pointed the same way, there's not much scope for disagreement.

The truth however, is near inevitably that there is only a very small minority making a disproportionate noise about their case. There is no debate over evolution, or the dinosaurian origin of birds, or that HIV leads to AIDS, or that climate is changing, or a great many others. That there are real, accredited scientists who do not think this is the case is not in doubt (sadly). But that this represents a real schism in the scientific community, that large numbers of researchers take these positions and that it occupies a significant amount of scientific research, or that there is good evidence for that position is certainly incorrect. One or two people arguing a point (and often doing so primarily in the media) does not make a debate.

This can be especially insidious in the media in fact—the creationists have an obvious agenda, anti-vaccinationists are often clearly misguided, but the media should be there to present an unbiased and fair report of the state of play. Unfortunately this seems to be often interpreted as "there are two sides, so both get equal time to make their case" (or "this is new so should have its voice heard"). However this is far from a fair representation when the overwhelming amount of evidence supports one position over the other (and even more so when one side is not even represented by experts in the field).

Not too long ago, I saw a US production on feathered dinosaurs that spent a good portion of its middle section on the alleged "debate" over the origin of birds. Each side was effectively represented by a couple of researchers who got a couple of minutes screen time to talk about the evidence for their position and against the other. I think a non-expert might have ended up siding with the researchers on the consensus side that birds are indeed dinosaurs, but I also think it might have been close.

What this failed to mention of course is that aside from the people shown, one would have struggled to find many more supporters of the idea that birds are not descended from dinosaurs, but that palaeontologists would be queuing round the block to support the other side. And oddly enough, the hundreds of papers and even entire books written on this subject and all the volumes of data and intricate evolutionary studies and fossil evidence are rather hard to summarise in two minutes for a lay audience. The representation on screen might have been "fair" and even "balanced" in the sense that it gave both sides an equal opportunity to present their case to the public, but was incorrect and unrepresentative of both the evidence and the consensus scientific position. A tiny minority that disagree is not a case to call something a debate or a controversy, and that fact that there are dissenters does not mean both positions are equally valid or should be presented as such (there are people on street corners claiming the world will end tomorrow, but they don't get half of the front page opposite "World to carry on as normal"). It might have been entirely unintentional, but this very much presented a major rift in the dinosaur research community which doesn't really exist and hypes this up as a drama that isn't there.

This for me seems like the opposite of what good journalism should be. Surely the point is to provide a representation of the true state of affairs rather than spin (even if unintentionally) the fact that there is disagreement as something that is effectively 50:50, when it's 99.9:00.1 or less. This can be humorous from an insider's position when one sees the media triumph a paper as "reigniting the debate over x" when in truth the researchers have looked at the paper, noted an obvious flaw or that it simply rehashes old and incorrect arguments or data, and carried on. The flipside of this is where there really is a scientific debate, in which case the debate is not reignited at all, but merely still going on, it has merely come to the attention of the press and public again which is not the same thing at all.

And so to the second major point here: there really are scientific debates ongoing. There are points in science over which there is profound disagreement between researchers and where there have been a great deal of careful, detailed and often impressive and original research and yet no consensus has been reached. We have lots of data but it's contradictory or confused or ambivalent and new techniques and investigations have failed to resolve it. One side might be correct or the other, or both, or neither. It can get heated (I've heard of, but never seen a fist fight at a conference, but I've seen the odd shouting match between delegates) and what's most intriguing is that for all that people will disagree, there's still a desire to find out. Disagreement can be profound, but collaboration to reach the answer generally trumps anything else.

There really are scientific debates out there and they can be most fascinating and full of drama. They can inspire researchers to new heights of originality and insight to develop methods and data that could solve the problem. To diminish this very essence of scientific process and collaboration (collect data, analyse, deduce) by conflating it with vastly exaggerated or fundamentally false claims of disagreement (often promoted by those with no interest in the truth, only their version of it) the media are regularly giving a very false impression of scientific research and the opinions of the scientific community. There is no need to dramatise and exaggerate every slight disagreement or blip as a huge crisis or blow-up, not least when there's plenty that would provide an interesting narrative of real disagreement and joint discovery. That this use of language then plays into the hands of those wishing to promote their unsubstantiated or flatly disproved "science" as being on an equal footing to these real discussions and of relevance to the scientific process only makes matters worse. The media when covering science should be presenting an honest view of the issues, not opening the door for pseudoscience to give itself false credibility.

Not every disagreement in science is a scientific debate, and a tiny but vocal minority should not be given parity without a parity of data and evidence.

Evolution Should Be Taught in Public Schools, Not Attacked

Laura H. Kahn

Laura H. Kahn is physician and research scholar at Princeton University's Program on Science and Global Society. Kahn specializes in issues of biodefense, pandemics, and public health.

Understanding evolution is critical to confronting the twenty-first century's microbiological challenges. We need to educate the next generation of scientists to give them the tools to develop novel treatments against antibiotic resistant bacteria, emerging viruses, and other deadly microbes. They need to understand how these microbes develop and change, which requires an understanding of evolution. Sadly, ensuring that evolution gets taught in public schools remains an uphill battle—especially since certain segments of society insist that religious doctrine, masquerading as science, be taught instead.

In the nineteenth century, the prevailing dogma was "spontaneous generation." It did nothing to prepare scientists and physicians to develop effective strategies against the infectious diseases that were killing untold numbers of people. Louis Pasteur, the French chemist who developed the rabies vaccine, was instrumental in disproving spontaneous generation and replacing it with the germ theory of disease. He helped to convince the world that invisible microbes caused disease, which led to a revolution in medicine and public health.

Changing people's minds against spontaneous generation was no small feat since it was the accepted theory at the time. The theory proposed that life could emerge from nonliving organic matter and explained why maggots suddenly emerged from rotting meat and how vermin magically appeared in stored grain. While based

"Why Evolution Should Be Taught in Public Schools," by Laura H. Kahn, Bulletin of the Atomic Scientists, November 12, 2007. Reprinted by permission.

| 110

on observation, it was wrong. Scientists had previously identified microbes, but they were generally viewed as the result rather than the cause of disease.

Pasteur began studying spontaneous generation in 1859, around the same time he began studying fermentation. During this work, he discovered that yeasts were responsible for making wine palatable and bacteria was responsible for turning wine bad. Subsequent work on silkworms showed that microbes caused their illness and death. Pasteur saw the connection between microbes, fermentation, putrefaction, and disease. The challenge was to convince the scientific community, particularly the medical profession, to accept this novel idea.

Almost simultaneously with Pasteur, Felix-Archimede Pouchet, the director of the Museum of Natural History in Rouen, claimed to the Paris Academy of Sciences that he had produced spontaneous generation. He followed this declaration with *Heterogenie*, a 700-page book in which he claimed to prove that life could originate from inanimate matter.

Pasteur, a devout Catholic, initially believed in spontaneous generation, but his work on fermentation convinced him otherwise. Against the advice of his colleagues, he decided to jump into the debate against Pouchet, carefully planning his experiments to disprove Pouchet's claim.

Spontaneous generation proponents believed that exposure to air was the key factor in the generation of life. Pasteur devised experiments using a novel "swan-neck" flask that would address the issue. The swan neck allowed exposure to air but trapped microbes in the elongated, S-shaped glass neck. Pasteur conducted experiments in cellars, on mountains, and even on Swiss glaciers to show that different concentrations of microbes existed depending on location and elevation.

The controversy began to take on religious overtones as the debate caught the public's attention; people took sides based on prejudiced beliefs rather than factual evidence. Pouchet and his colleagues attempted to duplicate Pasteur's results without success. Pasteur demanded that the Academy of Sciences appoint a commission to repeat the experiments; Pouchet demanded an experimental match be conducted in a laboratory in the Museum of Natural History.

An eloquent debater, Pasteur came prepared with more than 50 flasks, some of which he had previously opened on mountains and had remained sterile. He proceeded to open others throughout the museum amphitheater with many remaining sterile. The academy issued an official announcement that Pasteur had successfully disproved spontaneous generation. But despite his triumph, proponents of spontaneous generation in other countries continued to attack his findings. Time and additional research by other scientists such as the German physician Robert Koch, who proved the bacterial cause of a number of infectious diseases, eventually put spontaneous generation to rest. For the first time in history, the new "germ theory of disease" allowed people to understand the nature of epidemics and to develop effective preventive and control strategies against infectious diseases.

Creationism Versus Evolution

"Creationism," the belief that a deity created the heavens, Earth, and all its living creatures, dates back to antiquity. Indeed, many civilizations have creation stories rooted in religious beliefs. Charles Darwin's "theory of evolution" generated considerable controversy because it threatened religious doctrine. (It still does.) However, unlike spontaneous generation, which was based on observation, creationism is based on belief.

Developing a scientific theory requires collecting data, conducting experiments, and generating hypotheses to explain natural phenomena. Darwin developed his theory after collecting extensive data while on a five-year, round-the-world journey aboard the HMS *Beagle*; Pasteur disproved spontaneous generation because it was a scientific theory based on observation.

Proponents of creationism insist that it's a scientific theory and that evolution doesn't explain phenomenon such as the development of multi-celled animals like apes, elephants, and horses from single-celled life-forms. They propose that creationism is an alternative scientific theory to evolution, yet they don't provide scientific evidence for the existence of an intelligent deity. Instead, they cite gaps in evolutionary theory.

Indeed, how would someone prove by observation and experimentation the existence of a deity? Or alternatively, how would someone disprove evolution? There's extensive evidence in the fossil record, in the genetic code, and in rapidly evolving microbes. There are also experimental results of thousands of years of human genetic manipulation through selective breeding of domesticated plants and animals. For example, human genetic modification has led to dog breeds that never would have evolved naturally. Yorkshire terriers, chihuahuas, and pugs don't resemble the wolves from which they evolved. And without attentive human care, these animals wouldn't stand a chance of surviving in the wilderness.

The first public debate on creationism versus evolution took place in 1860 at the British Association for the Advancement of Science between Thomas Huxley, who supported evolution, and Bishop Samuel Wilberforce who opposed it. The Scopes Monkey Trial was the first famous courtroom battle. (Notice none of these discussions included competing experiments or any scientific endeavors.) In 1925, Tennessee passed the Butler Act, which prohibited teaching evolution in public schools. The ACLU subsequently decided to defend any teacher who violated the Tennessee law, eventually recruiting John Scopes, a teacher at the Rhea County High School who discussed evolution with his biology class.

Judge John Raulston didn't allow expert scientific testimony during the trial. William Jennings Bryan served as the lawyer for the prosecution, and Clarence Darrow was the defense lawyer. The trial became a media circus. Ultimately, Scopes was convicted and fined $100. But in 1927, the Tennessee Supreme Court overturned the conviction. Tennessee repealed the Butler Act in 1967, but creationism proponents wouldn't let the issue rest.

In the early 1980s, Louisiana passed a creationism law prohibiting the teaching of evolution in public schools without also teaching creationism. Parents of Louisiana public schoolchildren, religious leaders, and teachers challenged the law. The case went to the US Supreme Court, which ruled in 1989 that the act violated the First Amendment. Despite the ruling, in 1999, the Kansas Board of Education cut evolution from its curriculum. Meanwhile, similar challenges were occurring in other states. In 2004, the Dover Area School Board in Harrisburg, Pennsylvania, adopted a policy that required high school students to be informed of creationism. Eleven parents sued. A judge subsequently ruled that teaching creationism was unconstitutional. While this was a victory for the separation of church and state in school science curricula, concern should remain regarding future attacks against teaching evolution in public schools. It's important to note that in the 1989 Supreme Court decision, Antonin Scalia and the late William Rehnquist dissented with the majority opinion. The Supreme Court now has a different composition, and future challenges to teaching evolution in public schools might be ruled differently.

According to a 2005 Harris Poll, a majority of US citizens believe in creationism. Another survey by the Pew Forum on Religion and Public Life found that two-thirds of Americans believe that creationism should be taught alongside evolution. These results demonstrate a failure of the educational system to teach science in public schools. With No Child Left Behind focusing on test results, science is getting even less attention now. This could result in US students graduating from public schools scientifically illiterate. Today's defenders of evolution should be just as dogged and diligent as Pasteur was in preventing a backslide against scientific progress and understanding.

Similar to how germ theory of disease allows us to understand the causes of infectious disease and the spread of epidemics, evolution allows us to understand the development of antimicrobial resistance, the potential of the avian influenza virus to mutate into a human pandemic influenza virus, and the emergence of novel pathogens that can infect plants, animals, and humans. In the dark ages, people believed that divine wrath caused disease. We have come a long way since, but we need to remain vigilant that our children receive a good science education to further enhance human understanding. And a good science education includes learning about evolution.

Religious Exemption for Vaccination Is Not Good Public Policy

Joe Lawlor

Joe Lawlor is a newspaper veteran and staff writer for the Portland Press Herald.

By a single vote, the state Senate this week preserved a religious exemption to vaccination requirements for children to enter Maine schools, even though no major religious organizations advocate in favor of skipping vaccinations.

The contentious vaccine bill is expected to be back for debate in the Maine House and Senate next week, at a time when the state has dangerously low rates of vaccination coverage among schoolchildren and parts of the nation are grappling with measles outbreaks.

Four Democratic senators joined all Republicans on Thursday to maintain the religious exemption in current law in an 18-17 vote on an amendment by Sen. David Miramant, D-Camden. The House voted in April for a version of the bill that removes all non-medical exemptions—philosophic and religious—to vaccinations needed to attend school and day care.

The discrepancy between the bills means lawmakers will be grappling with how to handle the little-used religious exemption. Ninety percent of vaccine opt-outs in 2018-19 used the philosophic exemption.

Catholics, Protestants, Jews and Muslims all encourage their followers to be immunized against communicable diseases such as measles, chickenpox and whooping cough. Small subsets of religions, such as ultra-Orthodox Jews in New York City, may cite religious reasons for not vaccinating, although rabbis in New York have been encouraging the population to immunize. New York

"Religious Exemption to Vaccination Wouldn't Be Keeping the Faith," by Joe Lawlor, Press Herald, May 4, 2019. Reprinted by permission.

City has had at least 423 measles cases since October, according to city public health statistics.

Religion was often cited in the news as a reason for the 2015 measles outbreak in Amish communities in Ohio. But a 2017 scholarly article in the *American Journal for Infection Control* found that religion was not a major factor among parents who chose to forgo vaccines for their children, but rather misinformation about vaccine safety led to low vaccination rates among the Amish in 2015.

Rev. Jim Gertmenian, a retired United Church of Christ pastor from Cumberland, said that mainline Protestant and Catholic church teachings support vaccination. He said using religion as a catch-all reason to avoid vaccines that benefit the health of the community is false logic.

"That would be like saying 'God doesn't want me to obey traffic signals, and that is my sincere religious belief,'" Gertmenian said. "At some point, the state needs to step in for the betterment of the community."

Miramant, the sponsor of the amendment, said in an email Friday night that the religious exemption is important because, for some, there are "reasons that are personal to them and their God. Our Constitution grants the right and freedom of religious practice and I believe we must not start to let others define that intimate connection."

Carroll Conley, executive director of the Christian Civic League of Maine, made a similar point when he testified against the vaccine bill in March, saying that the "absence of a specific doctrine" by religious groups does not mean the state can infringe upon people's religious beliefs.

"Our opposition is based on the proposed bill's disregard for two bedrock foundations of America: religious freedom and parental rights," Conley said.

If the religious exemption in Maine is retained as it currently stands, parents would be able to forgo vaccines for schoolchildren by checking a box on a form, although another box on the same form—for the philosophic exemption—would be eliminated. Public health advocates fear that parents who were checking the philosophic exemption box on the form will instead check the religious box.

In Vermont, the religious exemption was little used until the philosophic exemption was eliminated in 2015. Religious opt-outs in Vermont jumped from 0.9 percent of all exemptions in 2015-16 to 3.7 percent in 2016-17, the first school year after the philosophic exemption was removed.

Maine's high rate of parents opting their children out of school-required vaccines—5.6 percent in 2018-19 for children entering kindergarten—spurred Democratic lawmakers to introduce a bill that would eliminate the philosophic and religious exemptions to vaccines. While the statewide average was 5.6 percent, in some schools the opt-out rate is much higher, which makes those communities more likely to experience the return of preventable diseases. Forty-three Maine elementary schools had kindergarten opt-out rates of 15 percent or more, well above the 5 percent threshold at which public health experts say the "herd immunity" that helps keep the diseases from circulating is threatened.

Maine's low vaccination rate also is likely contributing to the state's sky-high pertussis rate, public health experts say. Maine had 446 cases of pertussis, also known as whooping cough, in 2018, eight times higher than the national average, with many of the outbreaks occurring in schools.

While 0.2 percent of the non-medical exemptions in 2018-19 were for religious reasons, public health advocates say keeping the religious exemption creates a loophole that will let opt-out rates remain high.

"If you retain the religious exemption, you retain the risk. Religious exemptions seems to be a compromise, but in fact they will only compromise our public health as philosophical objectors switch to religious objectors," said Dr. Laura Blaisdell, a Yarmouth pediatrician and vaccine advocate.

What will happen next with the legislation is unclear. The House could send the original bill back to the Senate for a re-vote, Democratic leadership could try to flip one Democratic senator's vote, lawmakers could devise another compromise bill, the House could accept the Senate's version or no bill could be approved.

Sen. Linda Sanborn, D-Gorham, a retired physician, said she fears that as the bill stands after the Senate vote, parents will "switch to the religious exemption" even though it would be "illogical" to do so. But Sanborn said she and other lawmakers will be working on solutions in the upcoming weeks.

"I would like to think that all doors are not yet closed to us," Sanborn said.

States Help Themselves by Stopping Religious Exemption of Scientifically Proven Vaccinations

Bobby Allyn

Bobby Allyn is a business reporter based in San Francisco. Allyn has covered many breaking news stories for National Public Radio.

New York Gov. Andrew Cuomo signed a bill Thursday ending vaccination exemptions based on religious beliefs, the latest attempt to address the growing measles outbreak, the worst the US has experienced in decades.

Cuomo said plugging the loophole should help contain the spike in measles cases in New York, the state hardest hit by the uptick in the contagious virus due to low vaccination rates in ultra-Orthodox communities.

"The science is crystal clear: Vaccines are safe, effective and the best way to keep our children safe," Cuomo said after signing the bill. "While I understand and respect freedom of religion, our first job is to protect the public health and by signing this measure into law, we will help prevent further transmissions and stop this outbreak right in its tracks."

The Democratic-controlled Legislature approved the measure, which also eliminates other nonmedical exemptions for schoolchildren across the state.

"We are facing an unprecedented public health crisis," said Sen. Brad Hoylman, the legislation's sponsor. "The atrocious peddlers of junk science and fraudulent medicine who we know as anti-vaxxers have spent years sowing unwarranted doubt and fear, but it is time for legislators to confront them head-on."

The exemption, which exists in some form in most states, allows parents of schoolchildren to cite their religious beliefs in

"New York Ends Religious Exemptions for Required Vaccines," by Bobby Allyn, National Public Radio, June 13, 2019. Reprinted by permission.

opting their kids out of required vaccines. Supporters of keeping the religious exemptions say religious freedom should not be overpowered by state laws.

After the final vote tally was announced in the assembly, howling protesters, including the parents of unvaccinated children, filled the chamber, hurling expletives and chanting "shame on you" until lawmakers moved to recess.

Some backers of the bill have seen the measles outbreak up close, both in their districts and in their own homes, such as Assembly member Kenneth Zebrowski, who represents Rockland County. There, he noted, there have already been more than 266 confirmed measles cases, including 16 hospitalizations.

His 1-year-old daughter had to get her first vaccine shot at 6 months of age before her regularly scheduled immunization when she turned 1 recently.

"We had to get our kids overvaccinated," he said of his and other families in the district. "Because of this epidemic. I'm not particularly thrilled."

To those who question whether the recent measles outbreak in New York is indeed an epidemic, Zebrowski said that should not be the focus. The job of lawmakers, he said, is not to react to epidemics.

"Our job as legislators is to prevent epidemics," he said.

The Centers for Disease Control and Prevention reported last week that the number of new measles cases this year has exceeded 1,000, the highest count in 27 years.

Most of those new measles cases have been concentrated in ultra-Orthodox areas of New York, including Rockland County and parts of Brooklyn, adding urgency to the statewide debate around religious exemptions to vaccines.

The New York Assembly narrowly passed the bill by a 77-53 vote. It needed 76 votes for passage. Lawmakers in the state Senate advanced the measure by a tally of 36-26.

A small number of other states, including California, Mississippi and Arizona, have already passed laws banning vaccine exemptions on religious grounds. (Arizona law currently allows for a parent to opt a child out of mandatory vaccinations because of "personal beliefs," but not on religious grounds. A proposed bill in the Arizona Legislature had sought to expand the vaccination exemptions to include religious beliefs, but it has stalled.)

In New York, about 96% of students have been immunized against measles, mumps and rubella, yet "a measles outbreak continues to affect communities in several parts of the state where the rate is lower," according to state health officials.

In the 2017-2018 school year, 26,217 students in New York, including those in public and private schools and children in day care and prekindergarten, had religious exemptions from vaccinations, officials said.

"Although the state can claim high immunization rates overall, preventable diseases like measles remain a public health threat when administrative loopholes allow children to go unvaccinated, carrying the potential to harm communities—and especially our most vulnerable residents," said Dr. Howard Zucker, the commissioner of the state Department of Health.

New York state Sen. John Liu, who represents Queens, said while he thinks removing the religious exemption is the right move, he has heard from constituents who hold "deep and sincere" religious beliefs who would be "absolutely outraged that anyone would suggest that they don't care about the health of their children." Liu suggested that the tenor of the debate on both sides could be more civil. "We can respectfully disagree," Liu said.

The law eliminating religious exemptions takes effect immediately. Unvaccinated students will have up to 30 days to show school officials they have received their first dose of each required immunization.

In April, New York City health officials declared a public health emergency because of the measles outbreak. Parents of unvaccinated children could be fined $1,000 for not complying with the order.

Regulation of Generic Drug Manufacture Is Not Effective

C. Michael White

C. Michael White is a professor and head of pharmacy practice at the University of Connecticut.

Generic prescription drugs have saved the US about US$1.7 trillion over the past decade. The Food and Drug Administration approved a record 781 new generics in 2018 alone, including generic versions of Cialis, Levitra and Lyrica. They join generic versions of blockbusters from yesteryear, like Lipitor, Nexium, Prozac and Xanax.

Seniors are the biggest purchasers of generics, because they take the most medications and are on fixed incomes, but virtually everyone has taken a generic antibiotic or pain pill at one time.

This leads to a vital question: Are generics safe? If drug manufacturers followed the FDA's strict regulations, the answer would be a resounding yes. Unfortunately for those who turn to generics to save money, the FDA relies heavily on the honor system with foreign manufacturers, and US consumers get burned. Eighty percent of the active ingredients and 40% of the finished generic drugs used in the US are manufactured overseas.

As a pharmacist, I know that the safety of prescription medications is vital. My research, recently published in the *Annals of Pharmacotherapy*, raises alarming concerns about our vulnerabilities.

Where Are Your Drugs Being Made?

Generic drug manufacturers either make bulk powders with the active ingredient in them or buy those active ingredients from other companies and turn them into pills, ointments or injectable products.

In 2010, 64% of foreign manufacturing plants, predominantly in India and China, had never been inspected by the FDA. By 2015, 33% remained uninspected. In addition, companies in other countries are informed before an inspection, giving them time to clean up a mess. Domestic inspections are unannounced.

Faking Results

As I detail in my paper, when announced foreign FDA inspections began to occur in earnest between 2010 and 2015, numerous manufacturing plants were subsequently barred from shipping drugs to the US after the inspections uncovered shady activities or serious quality defects. Unscrupulous foreign producers shredded documents shortly before FDA visits, hid documents offsite, altered or manipulated safety or quality data or utilized unsanitary manufacturing conditions. Ranbaxy Corporation pleaded guilty in 2013 to shipping substandard drugs to the US and making intentionally false statements. The company had to withdraw 73 million pills from circulation, and the company paid a $500 million fine.

These quality and safety issues can be deadly. In 2008, 100 patients in the US died after receiving generic heparin products from foreign manufacturers. Heparin is an anticoagulant used to prevent or treat blood clots in about 10 million hospitalized patients a year and is extracted from pig intestines. Some of the heparin was fraudulently replaced with chondroitin, a dietary supplement for joint aches, that had sulphur groups added to the molecule to make it look like heparin. One of the heparin manufacturers inspected by the FDA received a warning letter after it was found to have used raw material from uncertified farms, used storage equipment with unidentified material adhering to it and had insufficient testing for impurities.

These issues continue to this day. Dozens of blood-pressure and anti-ulcer drugs were recalled in 2018 and 2019 due to contamination with the potentially carcinogenic compounds N-nitrosodimethylamine or N-nitrosodiethylamine. One of the major producers of these active ingredient powders used by multiple generic manufacturers was inspected in 2017. The FDA found that the company fraudulently omitted failing test results and replaced them with passing scores. This raises a critical question: How many more violations would occur with inspections occurring as frequently as they do in the US, and more importantly, if they were unannounced? Relatively speaking, the number of drugs proved to be tainted or substandard has been small, and the FDA has made some progress since 2010. But the potential for harm is still great.

What's Next?

How safe should US residents feel when 80% of the active ingredients in our drugs are made overseas? Evidence shows that the FDA can't trust the documents that foreign manufacturers produce to ensure that their products meet quality standards. The widespread willingness of foreign manufacturers to falsify, manipulate or shred documents in order to sell lower-quality or unsafe drugs to US citizens shows that only frequent unannounced FDA inspections or FDA testing of batches of medications when they reach the US will compel them to follow the rules.

Patients taking prescription drugs are sick and vulnerable; they should not be subjected to poor-quality medications that can make them worse. Similarly, domestic generic drug manufacturers employing US citizens should not have to face strict regulatory compliance that effectively is not required of foreign competitors.

It is expensive, logistically challenging and politically unpalatable for the FDA to show up for unannounced inspections of foreign plants. If the agency is not given that right or the funding to ramp up testing of their products here in the US, it should not be subjecting US citizens to the drugs produced in foreign plants. Unless we tackle this issue soon, I am afraid there will be a major incident where patients are killed and the golden goose—those immense savings associated with generic drugs—will also be sacrificed.

Unregulated Artificial Intelligence Will Cause Mass Unemployment

Quincy Larson

Quincy Larson is a teacher who founded FreeCodeCamp for people to learn how to computer code.

The automation of factories has already decimated jobs in traditional manufacturing, and the rise of artificial intelligence is likely to extend this job destruction deep into the middle classes, with only the most caring, creative or supervisory roles remaining."—Stephen Hawking

There's a rising chorus of concern about how quickly robots are taking away human jobs.

Here's Elon Musk on Thursday at the the World Government Summit in Dubai:

> What to do about mass unemployment? This is going to be a massive social challenge. There will be fewer and fewer jobs that a robot cannot do better [than a human]. These are not things that I wish will happen. These are simply things that I think probably will happen.

And today Bill Gates proposed that governments start taxing robot workers the same way we tax human workers:

> You cross the threshold of job-replacement of certain activities all sort of at once. So, you know, warehouse work, driving, room cleanup, there's quite a few things that are meaningful job categories that, certainly in the next 20 years [will go away].

Jobs are vanishing much faster than anyone ever imagined.

In 2013, policy makers largely ignored two Oxford economists who suggested that 45% of all US jobs could be automated away within the next 20 years. But today that sounds all but inevitable.

"A Warning from Bill Gates, Elon Musk, and Stephen Hawking," by Quincy Larson, freeCodeCamp.org, February 19, 2017. Reprinted by permission.

Transportation and Warehousing Employ 5 Million Americans

Those self-driving cars you keep hearing about are about to replace a lot of human workers.

Currently in the US, there are:

- 600,000 Uber drivers
- 181,000 taxi drivers
- 168,000 transit bus drivers
- 505,000 school bus drivers

There's also around 1 million truck drivers in the US. And Uber just bought a self-driving truck company.

As self driving cars become legal in more states, we'll see a rapid automation of all of these driving jobs. If a one-time $30,000 truck retrofit can replace a $40,000 per year human trucker, there will soon be a million truckers out of work.

And it's not just the drivers being replaced. Soon entire warehouses will be fully automated.

I strongly recommend you invest 3 minutes in watching this video: https://youtu.be/8gy5tYVR-28. It shows how a fleet of small robots can replace a huge number of human warehouse workers.

There are still some humans working in those warehouses, but it's only a matter of time before some sort of automated system replaces them, too.

8 Million Americans Work as Retail Salespeople and Cashiers

Many of these jobs will soon be automated away.

Amazon is testing a type of store with virtually no employees. You just walk in, grab what you want, and walk out.

A big part of sales is figuring out—or even predicting—what a customer will want. Well, Amazon grossed $136 billion last year, and its "salespeople" are its algorithm-powered recommendation engines. Imagine the impact that Amazon will have on retail when they release all of that artificial intelligence into brick-and-mortar stores.

US Restaurants Employ 14 Million People

Japan has been automating aspects of its restaurants for decades—taking orders, serving food, washing dishes, and even food preparation itself.

And America is now getting some automated restaurants as well.

There's even a company that makes delivery trucks that drive around and start baking pizzas in real time as orders come in.

Automation Is Inevitable. But We Still Have Time to Take Action and Help Displaced Workers.

Automation is accelerating. The software powering these robots becomes more powerful every day. We can't stop it. But we can adapt to it.

Bill Gates recommends we tax robotic workers so that we can recapture some of the money displaced workers would have paid as income tax.

Elon Musk recommends we adopt universal basic income and give everyone a certain amount of money each year so we can keep the economy going even as millions of workers are displaced by automation.

And I recommend we take some of the taxpayer money we're using to subsidize industries that are now mostly automated, and instead invest it in training workers for emerging engineering jobs.

The answer to the automation challenge may involve some combination of these three approaches. But we need to take action now, before we face the worst unemployment disaster since the Great Depression.

I strongly encourage you to do 3 things:

1. Educate yourself on the automation and its economics effects. This is the best book on the subject: *The Second*

Machine Age: Work, Progress, and Prosperity in a Time of Brilliant Technologies by Erik Brynjolfsson and Andrew McAfee.

2. Talk with your friends and family about automation. We can't ignore it just because it's scary and unpredictable. We need a public discourse on this so we can decide as a country what to do about it—before the corporations and their bottom lines decide for us.

3. Contact your representatives and ask them what they're doing about automation and unemployment. Tell them we need a robot tax, universal basic income, or more money invested into technology education—whichever of these best aligns with your political views.

If we act now, we can still rise to the automation challenge and save millions of Americans from hardship.

Scientific Experts Agree: Be Cautious with Artificial Intelligence

Tristan Greene

Tristan Greene is a reporter at the Next Web, where he writes about the advances of artificial intelligence and political policy surrounding technology.

When a panel of renowned AI experts was asked whether it would be possible for machines to develop superintelligence the answer was unanimous: yes. It seems like there's no longer a debate on whether computers will become more intelligent than humans, only when.

The panel, held earlier this year in California, was comprised of a "who's who" of science and philosophy in the AI space:

- Bart Selman (Cornell)
- David Chalmers (NYU)
- Elon Musk (Tesla, SpaceX)
- Jaan Tallinn (CSER/FLI)
- Nick Bostrom (FHI)
- Ray Kurzweil (Google)
- Stuart Russell (Berkeley)
- Sam Harris
- Demis Hassabis (DeepMind)

While it's theoretically possible, given what we understand about the laws of physics, for a computer to surpass human intelligence to the point in which the term "superintelligence" becomes applicable, surely the odds of that happening have to be slim to none. Right?

It's actually likely, according to every member of that panel. When asked to answer the question "is it likely AI will reach

"Stephen Hawking Thinks AI Will Cure Disease if It Doesn't Kill Us All," by Tristan Greene, The Next Web, November 7, 2017. Reprinted by permission.

superintelligence" with a yes, no, or "it's complicated" each member responded "yes."

Elon Musk even pretended to disagree with the other panelists, much to the delight of the audience and a few of the brains on stage. Perhaps because there's an awkwardness that happens when extremely intelligent people are entirely on the same page; it's hard to do science without debate.

Superintelligence?

If we're reconciled to the idea AI will reach "superintelligence" it's time we understood what that means and when it's going to happen.

Professor Nick Bostrom is the guy who literally wrote the book on superintelligence. In his text, aptly named *Superintelligence*," he defines the concept as "a hypothetical agent that possesses intelligence far surpassing that of the brightest and most gifted human minds."

It'll be smarter than we are, which means we won't be able to understand it then—and we certainly can't now.

The obvious truth about AI is that no one can predict what's going to happen in the long term. It's arguable that machine-learning advances are occurring so quickly it may be naive to think we know what's going to happen in the next six months.

We're in uncharted territory.

But what's any of this got to do with Stephen Hawking?

Professor Hawking, in a recent interview in *Wired* magazine, says AI is a technological revolution:

> Perhaps with the tools of this new technological revolution, we will be able to undo some of the damage done to the natural world by the last one—industrialization. And surely we will aim to finally eradicate disease and poverty. Every aspect of our lives will be transformed. In short, success in creating AI could be the biggest event in the history of our civilization.

He isn't the only one who believes AI will change our lives forever. Professor Nick Bostrom says AI represents the third "fundamental change in the human condition."

The Revolution

The first, according to Bostrom, was the agricultural revolution, which was followed by the industrial revolution. If AI exceeds human intelligence, we'll reach the next technological revolution.

It can be very difficult to reckon the "fact" that AI is going to have an impact as big as the industrial revolution—especially since most of the headlines read like science-fiction horror.

Professor Hawking, in the same interview, also said:

> I fear that AI may replace humans altogether. If people design computer viruses, someone will design AI that improves and replicates itself. This will be a new form of life that outperforms humans.

Professor Hawking probably wasn't suggesting that we cease researching AI and become Luddites.

It's simply easier to wrap our heads around the idea of killer robots taking over the world. We've seen that movie a dozen times already. Futhermore, a vision of the future is always easier to see through a lens of destruction, otherwise it's distorted by reality.

The world of tomorrow, that cinema and science-fiction have painted, is typically one that looks like today, but with cooler gadgets and adolescent-quality slang. Trying to explain what a world that's been revolutionized by artificial intelligence will really look like is a difficult endeavor.

Professor Bostrom, earlier this month, told member's of UK Parliament's artificial intelligence committee that there's simply no way to do that:

> As with any new general purpose technology it might very well be that the most exciting applications are not obvious at the outset, and are only discovered as people can start to play with the technology.

Headlines that tell us Stephen Hawking and Elon Musk think AI could destroy the human race are the fast-food version of the actual conversations, quite often.

The real calories lie in the excitement and longing optimism that Musk and Hawking both dish out concerning machine-learning technology. Professor Hawking believes AI could cure disease. Musk is heavily involved in Open AI, a foundation whose mission states:

> Artificial general intelligence (AGI) will be the most significant technology ever created by humans.

Hyperbole and fear will make naysayers of us all, if we only let them. The more practical approach—the one even Elon "AI Will Start WWIII" Musk seems to be taking—is to move forward with caution, optimism, and the best interests of all humankind in mind.

Questioning May Be Valid in Cases of Scientific Misconduct

National Academies Press

The National Academies Press publishes more than 200 books a year with titles covering science, engineering, and medicine.

Beyond honest errors and errors caused through negligence are a third category of errors: those that involve deception. Making up data or results (fabrication), changing or misreporting data or results (falsification), and using the ideas or words of another person without giving appropriate credit (plagiarism)—all strike at the heart of the values on which science is based. These acts of scientific misconduct not only undermine progress but the entire set of values on which the scientific enterprise rests. Anyone who engages in any of these practices is putting his or her scientific career at risk. Even infractions that may seem minor at the time can end up being severely punished.

The ethical transgressions discussed in earlier sections—such as misallocation of credit or errors arising from negligence—are matters that generally remain internal to the scientific community. Usually they are dealt with locally through the mechanisms of peer review, administrative action, and the system of appointments and evaluations in the research environment. But misconduct in science is unlikely to remain internal to the scientific community. Its consequences are too extreme: it can harm individuals outside of science (as when falsified results become the basis of a medical treatment), it squanders public funds, and it attracts the attention of those who would seek to criticize science. As a result, federal agencies, Congress, the media, and the courts can all get involved. Within the scientific community, the effects of misconduct—in

Institute of Medicine, National Academy of Sciences, and National Academy of Engineering. 1995. *On Being a Scientist: Responsible Conduct in Research*, Second Edition. https://doi.org/10.17226/4917. Reprinted with permission of the National Academy of Sciences, Courtesy of the National Academies Press, Washington, DC.

terms of lost time, forfeited recognition to others, and feelings of personal betrayal—can be devastating. Individuals, institutions, and even entire research fields can suffer grievous setbacks from instances of fabrication, falsification, or plagiarism even if they are only tangentially associated with the case.

When individuals have been accused of scientific misconduct in the past, the institutions responsible for responding to those accusations have taken a number of different approaches. In general, the most successful responses are those that clearly separate a preliminary investigation to gather information from a subsequent adjudication to judge guilt or innocence and issue sanctions if necessary. During the adjudication stage, the individual accused of misconduct has the right to various due process protections, such as reviewing the evidence gathered during the investigation and cross-examining witnesses.

In addition to falsification, fabrication, and plagiarism, other ethical transgressions directly associated with research can cause serious harm to individuals and institutions. Examples include cover-ups of misconduct in science, reprisals against whistleblowers, malicious allegations of misconduct in science, and violations of due process in handling complaints of misconduct in science. Policymakers and scientists have not decided whether such actions should be considered misconduct in science—and therefore subject to the same procedures and sanctions as falsification, fabrication, and plagiarism—or whether they should be investigated and adjudicated through different channels. Regulations adopted by the National Science Foundation and the Public Health Service define misconduct to include "other serious deviations from accepted research practices," in addition to falsification, fabrication, and plagiarism, leaving open the possibility that other actions could be considered misconduct in science. The problem with such language is that it could allow a scientist to be accused of misconduct for using novel or unorthodox research methods, even though such methods are sometimes needed to proceed in science. Federal officials respond by saying that this language is needed to prosecute ethical breaches that do not strictly fall into the categories of falsification, fabrication, or plagiarism and that no scientist has been accused of misconduct on the basis of using unorthodox research methods. This area of science policy is still evolving.

Fabrication in a Grant Application

Don is a first-year graduate student applying to the National Science Foundation for a predoctoral fellowship. His work in a lab where he did a rotation project was later carried on successfully by others, and it appears that a manuscript will be prepared for publication by the end of the summer. However, the fellowship application deadline is June 1, and Don decides it would be advantageous to list a publication as "submitted." Without consulting the faculty member or other colleagues involved, Don makes up a title and author list for a "submitted" paper and cites it in his application.

After the application has been mailed, a lab member sees it and goes to the faculty member to ask about the "submitted" manuscript. Don admits to fabricating the submission of the paper but explains his actions by saying that he thought the practice was not uncommon in science.

The faculty members in Don's department demand that he withdraw his grant application and dismiss him from the graduate program. After leaving the university, Don applies for a master's degree, since he has fulfilled the course requirements. Although the department votes not to grant him a degree, the university administration does so because it is not stated in the university graduate bulletin that a student in Don's department must be in "good standing" to receive a degree. They fear that Don will bring suit against the university if the degree is denied. Likewise, nothing will appear in Don's university transcript regarding his dismissal.

1. Do you agree with Don that scientists often exaggerate the publication status of their work in written materials?

2. Do you think the department acted too harshly in dismissing Don from the graduate program?

3. Do you believe that being in "good standing" should be a prerequisite for obtaining an advanced degree in science? If Don later applied to a graduate program at another institution, does that institution have the right to know what happened?

Another category of behaviors—including sexual or other forms of harassment, misuse of funds, gross negligence in a person's professional activities, tampering with the experiments of others or with instrumentation, and violations of government research regulations—are not necessarily associated with scientific conduct. Institutions need to discourage and respond to such behaviors. But these behaviors are subject to generally applicable legal and social penalties and should be dealt with using the same procedures that would be applied to anyone.

A Case of Plagiarism

May is a second-year graduate student preparing the written portion of her qualifying exam. She incorporates whole sentences and paragraphs verbatim from several published papers. She does not use quotation marks, but the sources are suggested by statements like "(see . . . for more details)." The faculty on the qualifying exam committee note inconsistencies in the writing styles of different paragraphs of the text and check the sources, uncovering May's plagiarism.

After discussion with the faculty, May's plagiarism is brought to the attention of the dean of the graduate school, whose responsibility it is to review such incidents. The graduate school regulations state that "plagiarism, that is, the failure in a dissertation, essay, or other written exercise to acknowledge ideas, research or language taken from others" is specifically prohibited. The dean expels May from the program with the stipulation that she can reapply for the next academic year.

1. Is plagiarism like this a common practice?

2. Are there circumstances that should have led to May's being forgiven for plagiarizing?

3. Should May be allowed to reapply to the program?

CHAPTER 4

Are Attacks on Science a Recent Phenomenon?

Overview: Are Scientists Responsible for Correcting Pseudoscience?

Rod Lamberts and Will J. Grant

Rod Lamberts is the deputy director for the Australian National Center for Public Awareness of Science at the Australian National University. Will J. Grant is a researcher and lecturer at the Australian National University.

The ABC's [Australian Broadcasting Corporation] flagship science journalism TV programme, *Catalyst*, has riled the scientific community once again. And, in a similar vein to *Catalyst*'s controversial 2013 report on the link between statins, cholesterol and heart disease, it has now turned its quasi-scientific attention to a supposed new peril.

Its "Wi-Fried?" segment last week raised concerns about the ever-increasing "electronic air pollution" that surrounds us in our daily lives, exploiting a number of age-old, fear-inspiring tropes.

There are already plenty of robust critiques of the arguments and evidence, so exploring where they got the science wrong is not our goal.

Instead, we're interested in using the segment as inspiration to revisit an ongoing question about scientists' engagement with the public: how should the scientific community respond to issues like this?

Should scientists dive in and engage head-on, appearing face-to-face with those they believe do science a disservice? Should they shun such engagement and redress bad science after the fact in other forums? Or should they disengage entirely and let the story run its course?

"Should Scientists Engage with Pseudo-Science or Anti-Science?" by Rod Lamberts and Will J. Grant, The Conversation Media Group Ltd, February 24, 2016. https://theconversation.com/should-scientists-engage-with-pseudo-science-or-anti-science-54953. Licensed under CC BY-ND 4.0.

There are many of examples of what scientists could do, but to keep it simple we focus here just on the responses to "Wi-Fried" by two eminent Professors, Simon Chapman and Bernard Stewart, both of whom declined to be a part of the ABC segment, and use this case to consider what scientists should do.

Just Say No

In an interview about their decision to not participate, Chapman and Stewart independently expressed concerns about the evidence, tone and balance in the "Wi-Fried" segment. According to Chapman it "contained many 'simply wrong' claims that would make viewers unnecessarily afraid."

Stewart labelled the episode "scientifically bankrupt" and "without scientific merit." He added:

> I think the tone of the reporting was wrong, I think that the reporter did not fairly draw on both sides, and I use the word "sides" here reluctantly.

Indeed, in situations like this, many suggest that by appearing in the media alongside people who represent fringe thinkers and bad science, respected experts lend them unwarranted credibility and legitimacy.

Continuing with this logic, association with such a topic would mean implicitly endorsing poor science and bad reasoning, and contribute to an un-evidenced escalation of public fears.

But Is It Really That Straightforward?

The concerns Chapman and Stewart expressed about the show could equally be used to argue that experts in their position should have agreed to be interviewed, if only to present a scientifically sound position to counter questionable claims.

In this line, you could easily argue it's better for experts to appear whenever and wherever spurious claims are raised, the better to immediately refute and dismiss them.

On the other hand, if scientific experts refuse to engage with "scientifically bankrupt" arguments, this could send a more potent message: that the fringe claims are irrelevant, not even worth wasting the time to refute. So this would mean they shouldn't engage with this kind of popular science story.

On the third hand, their refusal to engage could be re-framed to characterise the experts as remote, arrogant or even afraid, casting doubt on the veracity of the scientific position. So to avoid this impression, experts should engage.

But wait, there's more.

Participation in these kinds of popular science shows could also tarnish the reputation of the expert. But not appearing means missing the opportunity to thwart the potential harm caused by fringe, false or non-scientific claims.

And what about an expert's obligation to defend their science, to set the record straight, and to help ensure people are not misled by poor evidence and shonky reasoning? Is this best done by engaging directly with dubious media offerings like "Wi-Fried," or should relevant experts find other venues?

Should Scientists Engage Anti-Science?

Well, this depends on what they think they might achieve. And if one thing stands out in all the to-ing and fro-ing over what scientists should do in such cases, it's this: the majority of proponents both for and against getting involved seem convinced that popular representations of science will change people's behaviour.

But there is rarely any hard evidence presented in the myriad "scientists should" arguments out there. Sticking with the *Catalyst* example, there is really only one, far-from-convincing, study from 2013 suggesting the show has such influence.

If you really want to make a robust, evidence-based decision about what experts should do in these situations, don't start with the science being discussed. In the case of *Catalyst*, you'd start with research on the show's relationship with its audience(s).

- What kinds of people watch *Catalyst*?

- Why do they watch it?
- To what extent are their attitudes influenced by the show?
- If their attitudes are actually influenced, how long does this influence last?
- If this influence does last, does it lead people to change their behaviours accordingly?

Of course, we applaud the motives of people who are driven to set the scientific record straight, and especially by those who are genuinely concerned about public welfare.

But to simply assume, without solid evidence, that programmes like *Catalyst* push people into harmful behaviour changes is misguided at best. At worst, it's actually bad science.

Fake News and Populism Threaten Science and Scientists

Chloe Hill

Chloe Hill is a policy officer at the European Geosciences Union, the leading organization for Earth, planetary, and space science research in Europe.

The 2019 EGU General Assembly was a great success. Not only was it the largest in EGU history (with over 16,000 participants, 5,531 oral, 9,432 poster and 1,287 PICO presentations) but it also allowed scientists to connect geoscience and their research with global challenges and potential solutions. One of the highlights of this year's General Assembly was the high-level session on Science, Politics and European (dis)integration which welcomed two prestigious speakers: Ilaria Capua and Mario Monti.

Ilaria Capua is professor and the director of the One Health Center of Excellence at the University of Florida in the United States. She is a veterinarian by training, a researcher in virology and was a member of the Italian Parliament from 2013 until 2016.

Mario Monti is currently a lifetime member of the Italian Senate and the president of Bocconi University in Milan, Italy. He served as a European Commissioner from 1995 to 2004 and was the Prime Minister of Italy from 2011 to 2013.

From Virtuous to Vicious Circle

The session focused on two of the European Union's greatest threats, populism and fake news, and how these mounting threats could impact both researchers and scientific progress. Mario Monti opened the session by praising the EU's virtuous circle of economic growth, evidence-based enlightenment, leadership and long-term

"GeoPolicy: Fake News and Populism—a Threat to Science in Europe," by Chloe Hill, European Geosciences Union, May 20, 2019. https://blogs.egu.eu/geolog/2019/05/20/fake -news-and-populism-a-threat-to-science-in-europe/. Licensed under CC BY 4.0.

vision. However, he cautioned that this virtuous circle could be turning into a vicious circle with leadership giving way to political followership, personal interest, rejection of competence, short-termism and fake news.

He warned that a "rise in a mixture of populism, nationalism, sovereignism and protectionism [is having] an impact globally, in the EU and in individual countries" and has the potential to lead to less democracy, more demagogy, and less integration between nations.

The Threat of Fake News

Ilaria Capua's very personal presentation told her story and her battle with fake news. After starting her career as a virologist and working in a diverse team on a European project, she was elected as a member of the Italian Parliament. Through this story, Capua highlighted the very real threat of fake news to science, researchers and institutions alike.

"I can tell you that I am very, very concerned of the next threat that is going to become viral. And this threat is the fake news threat for science."

She warned the scientists in the audience, "Science, scientists and institutions are under attack. Our biggest risk is that our personal and institutional credibility is shaken." Despite this, she encouraged scientists to still get involved in outreach and share their research with the public because, "…we have challenges that scientists are going to have to answer. They are going to need to talk to policymakers."

Capua also talked about what she is doing on a personal level to fight fake news and help protect science and institutions, "The real reason I am here is because I have a mission B in life. Mission B is to advocate for you. This is about you. This is about us. I have been a victim of fake news and experienced the violence of slander and despair of reputational loss. I am concerned and afraid that what happened to me can happen to you and can happen to institutions.

My mission B is to advocate for scientific integrity and to support scientists when they are accused of crimes or misconduct."

Fighting the Rise of Populism

Encouraging integration and raising awareness about the threat of rising populism and fake news is vital but one of the first questions raised by the audience was "What can we, as average researchers, do to foster integration?"

"Be yourself and tell surrounding people who you are and how the EU relates to you. And what aspects in your activity would not be there, or not be there so productively, if the EU was not there [or] if the EU was undermined," Monti responded.

Most arguments for integration are more complex and harder to illustrate than the non-fact-based arguments used by populists to undermine integration. It is therefore "important to promote EU with the positives" whenever possible.

"I would like to see a science pride movement," stated Capua, focusing on the need to organize. "We need to continue to defend EU research and its values. We need to prepare because attacks will come and we need to develop strategies to maintain our credibility to engage with the public." She also encouraged scientists to communicate their research more effectively and "find new ways to engage with the public," highlighting the EGU's Artist in Residence as one innovative method.

The session made it clear that while fake news and populism might not be something that scientists think about on a daily basis, it is something that can have a severe impact on how research is undertaken. Mario Monti finished his presentation with a warning and a call to action which seems particularly relevant in the lead up to the EU Elections.

"The next victim, I'm afraid, is going to be you. You are the stakeholders of European integration. Don't forget that the status of the work you do, the multiplier in terms of impact, of application and of global resonance, has a lot to do with the persistence or the going backwards of European integration. So please mobilise!"

EGU's Call for a United Europe

The session culminated with EGU President Alberto Montanari releasing a statement of support for a united Europe. "The EGU firmly believes that threats to a united Europe are threats to scientific research."

Following the session's discussion, the EGU statement acknowledges fake news, populism and malicious state actors as key threats to European integration and science. It highlights both the value of research to European "prosperity, wellbeing and global standing" and the need to "work together, pooling complementary skills, expertise and infrastructure, and share data and information within an open and unified environment" to increase the effectiveness of research and meet global challenges.

It concludes by affirming the EGU's commitment to stand up "for international cooperation in science and taking a leading role within the scientific community in order to reduce barriers to scientific collaboration and cooperation across Europe."

The Safety of GMOs Is Being Monitored

Joanna Fantozzi

Joanna Fantozzi is a storyteller, journalist, and features writer.

Every day, we're bombarded with food labels claiming that certain products are healthier than others. Walk the aisles of a grocery store (or even read a restaurant menu) and you'll find yourself interpreting a dizzying array of health buzzwords like "low-fat," "all-natural," and, of course, "non-GMO."

While there are problems with many of these labels, the question of what a genetically modified organism, or GMO, is and whether it's bad for your health has proven to be an especially persistent one. "Humans like to put things in boxes; there's the 'natural' box and the 'unnatural' box," says Anastasia Bodnar, a plant geneticist and the policy director of the nonprofit plant-science organization Biology Fortified. "We know things like Diet Coke aren't natural, but [GMOs] are different. They look natural but have been altered in ways people don't understand." And that, it seems, scares us.

Starting in 2020, large companies that make bioengineered foods will have to label those products in some form, which may further solidify the popular belief that GMOs are unappealing Frankenfoods—and make "non-GMO" foods sound healthier and more natural by comparison. But that's very misleading. Here's what you need to know.

First Things First: What Exactly Is a GMO? Am I Eating Them Already?

Genetically modified organisms are defined by the World Health Organization as "organisms (i.e. plants, animals, or microorganisms) in which the genetic material (DNA) has been altered in a way that

"What Are GMOs and Are They Bad for Me?" by Joanna Fantozzi, Vice Media, July 21, 2018. Reprinted by permission.

does not occur naturally by mating and/or natural recombination." Selectively bred animals or plants are considered GMOs—and few people have problems with techniques like plant grafting—but what we're talking about here is using technology to alter genes. For clarity, we'll call it GE, for *genetically engineered*. This term specifically refers to using tools to cut and paste recombinant DNA in the laboratory. (Even the FDA prefers "genetically engineered" in this case.)

Produce like the Red Delicious apple or the Cavendish banana that have been around for decades are not GE, since those foods were created by selective crossbreeding. The first GE crop—the Flavr Savr tomato—wasn't introduced to the general market until 1994.

The cutting and pasting of DNA is "the process of being able to cut out a specific gene and recombine it back into the genome of a cell that you want to change," says Peggy Lemaux, crop biotechnologist at the University of California, Berkeley. While that might sound meddlesome, the results are no different from a plant that was genetically altered via selective breeding, and the process is much more precise. "We already accept so many plants and animals in our food that have been bred to be totally different than how they were in nature," Bodnar says. "Biotechnology is just another tool we can use."

GE foods have become a huge part of our scientific lexicon over the past two decades, but you won't actually find very many of them for purchase in the produce aisle. They're mostly used in refined forms like soybean oil and cornstarch in processed foods. Lemaux says only a few varieties of genetically engineered whole produce are on the market, including sweet corn, squash, papaya, and most recently, the non-browning Arctic apple, which made headlines because it was so novel. (The Flavr Savr tomato is no longer sold.)

The two most common GE crops on the market right now are those with BT insect protection, or *Bacillus thuringiensis*, a "naturally occurring soil bacterium" that protects crops from pests when they have the trait added to their genomes, and "Roundup-ready" crops, which have been designed to allow farmers to spray the weed-killing herbicide glyphosate (aka Roundup) without harming the crops. Today, 89 percent of corn crops grown in America contain genes tolerant to herbicide.

I Heard They're Bad for Me. Are GE Foods and GMOs Unhealthy?

In short, there's no reason to believe that genetically engineered foods are bad for your health. "People may fear that the genetic changes could directly interact with their own DNA and cause mutations in themselves or their future children," says Ruth MacDonald, a food and nutrition scientist at Iowa State University. These fears, MacDonald says, are directly related to genetic illiteracy. She says genetic mutations in current or future generations as a result of eating genetically engineered foods is "of course not possible."

"DNA that is consumed in food (note that all natural foods from plants or animals contain DNA—so we eat DNA all the time) is degraded and does not get 'absorbed' into the body intact," MacDonald says. "It therefore is not logical to think that food-derived DNA could interact with the human genome."

The American Cancer Society says, "There is no proof at this time that the genetically modified foods that are now on the market are harmful to human health or that they would either increase or decrease cancer risk because of the added genes." Still the ACS points out that lack of proof of harm is not the same thing as proof of safety, so experts need to continue to assess and study these foods.

Gerald Berkowitz, professor at the Agricultural Biotechnology Lab at the University of Connecticut, says "the evidence is fairly clear that there is no documented, refereed science supporting a human health risk." That's not to say we shouldn't be taking a critical look at their role in our food system, he adds: "When I look at GMOs in a broad context, there are many questions that the public should be asking. GMOs are very much reflective of big agriculture in the US [and] contribute to the industrialization of agriculture."

Anti-GMO websites list a plethora of so-called toxicity and health concerns related to GE product consumption, like autoimmune disorders, infertility, and even autism, that they say are strongly associated with the use of glyphosate, an herbicide used on GE crops. The scientists we spoke to, however, said that studies have not (yet) found any proof of these claims, and a 2012 updated report distributed by the American Medical Association's Council on Science and Public Health reconfirmed that "there is no evidence that unique hazards exist either in the use of rDNA techniques or in the movement of genes between unrelated organisms," but similarly to the American Cancer Society, they strongly encourage the FDA to "remain alert to new data on the health consequences of bioengineered foods and update its regulatory policies accordingly."

To take one claim: Yes, autism rates went up (there was a 15 percent jump between 2012 and 2014) at the same time that Roundup was increasingly used on crops, but correlation does not equal causation. A 2007 study published in the journal *Environmental Health Perspectives,* which examined the relationship between autism spectrum disorders and maternal proximity to farms that use pesticides (including glyphosate), failed to find a connection but said that the issue "should be further studied."

Furthermore, the 2016 report *Genetically Engineered Crops: Experiences and Prospects* released by the National Academies of Science, Engineering, and Medicine concluded that "the overall similarity in prevalence of autism spectrum disorder in the United Kingdom, where GE foods are rarely eaten, and in the United States, where GE foods are commonly eaten, suggests that the major rise in autism spectrum disorder is not associated with the consumption of GE foods."

[Our organization] reached out to the Non-GMO Project, a non-profit organization that produces the "Non-GMO Project Verified" label commonly seen in grocery stores, about their stance on the toxicity of GMOs, but they declined to comment.

There are a few reasons why certain GE foods aren't great for you, but it has nothing to do with their having been genetically altered. One reason is that GE crops are commonly used to make ingredients like corn syrup used in processed junk food, which, newsflash, isn't healthy.

Lemaux points out that a genetically engineered artichoke, for instance, is much less likely to be sold in major grocery stores than GE technology used for ingredients in processed junk food with name recognition. These foods "are being created by large companies that have to make money," Lemaux says. "The regulatory process for GMO crops can cost anywhere between $10 and $20 million. My team has created four genetically engineered cereal crops and none of them went anywhere because we can't afford it."

Ok, So You're Saying GE Foods and GMOs Won't Give Me Cancer, Either?

There's no evidence that GMOs cause cancer. One reason you've heard that, though, is that, as mentioned above, there are a lot of GE crops designed to be used with the herbicide glyphosate, the active ingredient in Roundup, which was labeled a "probable carcinogen" by the International Association for Cancer Research, a World Health Organization committee, in 2015.

The announcement that a product used on common crops could cause cancer created subsequent outrage and division in the scientific community and the public. In October 2017, Reuters claimed that the IARC appeared to have edited or deleted data that was at odds with its conclusion of glyphosate being a "probable carcinogen," while other critics claim that the IARC was looking at hazards (conditions that have the potential for harm), rather than risk assessment (the likelihood of those hazards actually causing harm). The WHO committee later released a report in

January 2018 denying that it changed the data and defending its original findings.

The claims of glyphosate toxicity have been thrust back into the spotlight recently with the ongoing court battle between DeWayne Johnson, a California man who is dying of non-Hodgkin's lymphoma, and Roundup maker Monsanto over claims that the agrochemical giant has "specifically gone out of its way to bully… and to fight independent researchers" over alleged connections between glyphosate-based products and cancer.

Johnson worked as a groundskeeper for a California school district and regularly sprayed Roundup on plants and flowers as part of his job—and he was sometimes sprayed with the chemical himself on windy days—before he was diagnosed with his illness. Monsanto's lawyers claim that non-Hodgkin's lymphoma "takes years to develop," so Johnson's health problems likely began well before he started working at the school.

The outcome of this contentious court case could be an indicator of how similar lawsuits related to the herbicide might go, the Associated Press reports.

The tentative scientific consensus is that glyphosate has been a largely successful replacement for other, more harmful pesticides and herbicides like cyanazine, which was banned in the United States for toxicity levels in drinking water.

MacDonald says that the average person's exposure to glyphosate doesn't only come from GE crops and is likely pretty small. "The field corn grown with glyphosate resistance goes into things like starches, oil, and fiber," MacDonald says. "You might eat those indirectly but they're highly refined. Are there traces of glyphosate? Yes, but there will be traces in many foods because glyphosate is widely used in agriculture, not just [GE foods]." It's used on more than 200 types of crops in California alone.

A 2014 review of studies from the University of California, Davis, and published in the *Journal of Animal Science*, found that the most direct consumers of GE crops—the livestock that eat genetically engineered feed—have suffered no "unexpected perturbations or disturbing trends in animal performance or health indicators."

As for direct carcinogenic effects on humans, scientists admit that there hasn't been enough rigorous research in people examining the correlation between GE crops and cancer, as the National Academies of Science, Engineering, and Medicine (NASEM) concluded in its 2016 report. However, data from the National Cancer Institute shows that numbers of deaths from the most common cancers have continued to either decrease or stabilize, even with the introduction of GE crops into the food system.

"The figures show that some cancers have increased and others decreased, but there is no obvious change in the patterns since GE crops were introduced into the United States food system," the NASEM report's authors conclude.

Are There Benefits to GE and GMO Foods?

There are. "There are thousands of interesting GE traits that could make a huge impact on disease resistance, nutrition, feed efficiency, and more," Bodnar says. "But the trait has to get through regulation, the food manufacturer, and the consumer before it will go to market. We have so few of these tools available right now that they've become overused, and pests have developed a resistance."

As mentioned above, there are very few whole GE foods on the market right now—the only ones you will find in your supermarket include three varieties of squash, sweet corn, papaya, and the Arctic apple. Scientists have been scrambling to cut through red tape to get their new GE technologies approved and improve the genetic diversity of bioengineered crops.

One example of the complications related to emerging GE technologies is the creation of the non-allergenic peanut. Bodnar says scientists created these allergy-resistant peanuts a decade ago, but you can't just put that product out on store shelves. You'd have to grow it in such a way that guaranteed no cross-contamination with regular peanuts, all the way from field to shelf. It's not impossible, but it is expensive.

The scientists we spoke with are cautiously optimistic about the future of GMOs, from the vitamin A-fortified "golden rice" that is currently being tested in the Philippines, to new advancements in genetically engineered livestock like hornless cattle (which make the animals less dangerous to humans), and, as you've probably read about, salmon that have been genetically engineered to grow twice as fast by being injected with a growth hormone.

"These salmon would be the first GE animal in the food supply," Bodnar says. "They've been in the regulatory process since 1995. You could do the same thing in different ways: You could genetically engineer the salmon or selectively breed them. It's the same end result, but people hear 'genetically engineered seafood' and they want no part of it."

Many scientists agree that GE technologies have a significant role to play in the future of agriculture and global nutrition (that is, if they can get over the hurdles of marketability and regulation), so why are "non-GMO" labels becoming more common on grocery store shelves and restaurant menus?

"It's a total market strategy," MacDonald says. "When you have people who think that [GMOs are] something to avoid and you can market your product to say it doesn't have them, then of course you'd use that to your advantage."

Fake News Opposes Informative Science

Tawana Kupe

Tawana Kupe is the vice-chancellor and principal at the University of Pretoria in South Africa.

Democracy and social progress die without science and fact-based knowledge. Science and facts are the foundational basis for rational and logical disputation and the possibility of reaching some truths.

Fake news, on the other hand, is a calculated assault on democratic freedoms.

The power of the notion of fake news and of its practitioners is demonstrated by how we have all quickly come to accept that there is a category of news called fake news. By doing so, we are running the real risk of being complicit in its legitimisation. My point is: if it's fake then it's not news. There is news, and then there is fake stuff, dodgy facts, distortions and lies.

So what's the connection between science, knowledge and facts?

What Makes Good Science

Science is one important means of producing knowledge and getting to what approximates the truth. Good science results from rigorous processes. Part of the rigour in science and knowledge creation is the peer review process, which is a means of ensuring not only the correctness of facts, but also transparency.

Science must generally also meet the test of replicability. These days data used in scientific experiments often also has to be preserved so it can be assessed or analysed if results are disputed. Ethical norms also govern scientific experiments to prevent harm.

"Why Science Matters So Much in the Era of Fake News and Fallacies," by Tawana Kupe, The Conversation Media Group, March 18, 2019. https://theconversation.com/why-science-matters-so-much-in-the-era-of-fake-news-and-fallacies-113298. Licensed CC BY-ND 4.0.

Science is not the absolute truth. Scientific findings are the beginning, not the end, of the quest for truth. Empirical data used in science that can be verified forms a sound basis for robust discussion, debate and decision-making. Science brings a degree of rationality that creates a higher probability that the best interest of society or the public interest will be taken into account in, for example, decision-making.

Science, then, is the habit of exercising the mind to help think through especially difficult and complex phenomena.

This makes science important in the exercise of democracy. This isn't possible without facts and information that enable—or aid—voters to make an informed choice in elections, for example, or help the making of sound policies that best promote the public interest. Science also enables discerning members of the public to make sense of their worlds and the world.

So-Called Fake News

Fake news, on other hand, is a set of at worst, manufactured or concocted facts that are a perversion of reality. It is the direct antithesis of science.

But fake news isn't new. It's as old as news itself and has a variety of aims, including propaganda and spin doctoring. It can be argued that the growth of spin doctoring in the 1990s is the precursor to the exponential growth of fakery. It has also been enabled by the decline of content that enriches public discourse in the context of commercialisation and concentration of media since the 1980s.

These developments led to a decline in the influence of public interest media or media that strikes the balance between commercial enterprise and the public good. And this has led to the reduction in the kind of news and media content that focuses on science.

Science journalism and investigative journalism, in particular, have seriously declined. This has meant that the ability to shine a light on the dark areas of lack of knowledge, superstition, and myths has seriously been diminished.

Specialist reporting is now confined to the content-rich ghettos of those who are highly educated or interested.

Another reason for the growth of fake news and its increasing influence is the loss of confidence in public institutions, including media institutions and the profession of journalism. Fakery has risen to fill the vacuum, driven by individuals and political organisations who position themselves as messiahs with instant solutions to multiple social crises. In their discourse knowledge institutions, science, facts, evidence, experts and reason or rationality are thrown out of the window as the sophistry of the elite.

The Role of Social Media

Digital technologies and social media have made it much easier to produce and disseminate fake news. It is a paradox: unprecedented scientific advances and technologies are enabling us to transcend traditional constraints of distribution and literally place information at people's fingertips. Yet these same technologies seem to facilitate more fake news and information that doesn't necessarily advance the public good.

In addition, social media largely exists outside the professional norms of fact checking and the use of evidence to support assertions, arguments and positions taken in relation to social phenomena.

Fact checking and peer review are more important than ever because of the reality that false information now flows freely. This can be extremely harmful, particularly in public health campaigns.

The attraction of fake news is its apparent simplicity. It has a ring of truth around its claims, even when these are outlandish, and its ability to seem to resonate with what people think are their life-worlds or everyday life. Its ability to reinforce stereotypes, including prejudices, makes a bad situation even worse.

Science, Facts and Knowledge Will Save Humanity

Science journalism and investigative journalism which seek to pursue the truth rather than just the reporting of events, are critically important in this age of fake news and fallacies.

It is not an exaggeration to say that the sustainability of the idea of humanity and the environment in the broadest sense of the word depends on science—or the respect for facts, evidence and experts.

Science that allows the public to have a nuanced understanding of life is important to building inclusive, open societies that enable public participation in decision making and progressive social agendas. Science disseminated in ways that are understood by the public and resonate with their life-worlds is important for building trust in reformed institutions and creating new forms of social cohesion in diverse societies.

Attacks on Science and Scientists Are Nothing New

Catholic Answers

Catholic Answers is a media ministry that has a mission to disseminate information about the Catholic Church and its teachings.

It is commonly believed that the Catholic Church persecuted Galileo for abandoning the geocentric (earth-at-the-center) view of the solar system for the heliocentric (sun-at-the-center) view.

The Galileo case, for many anti-Catholics, is thought to prove that the Church abhors science, refuses to abandon outdated teachings, and is not infallible. For Catholics, the episode is often an embarrassment. It shouldn't be. This tract provides a brief explanation of what really happened to Galileo.

Anti-Scientific?

The Church is not anti-scientific. It has supported scientific endeavors for centuries. During Galileo's time, the Jesuits had a highly respected group of astronomers and scientists in Rome. In addition, many notable scientists received encouragement and funding from the Church and from individual Church officials. Many of the scientific advances during this period were made either by clerics or as a result of Church funding.

Nicolaus Copernicus dedicated his most famous work, *On the Revolution of the Celestial Orbs,* in which he gave an excellent account of heliocentrism, to Pope Paul III. Copernicus entrusted a preface to Andreas Osiander, a Lutheran clergyman who knew that Protestant reaction to it would be negative, since Martin Luther seemed to have condemned the new theory. Ten years prior to Galileo, Johannes Kepler published a heliocentric work that expanded on Copernicus's work. As a result, Kepler also found

"The Galileo Controversy," by Nihil Obstat, Catholic Answers. www.catholic.com. Reprinted by permission.

opposition among his fellow Protestants for his heliocentric views and found a welcome reception among some Jesuits who were known for their scientific achievements.

Clinging to Tradition?

Anti-Catholics often cite the Galileo case as an example of the Church refusing to abandon outdated or incorrect teaching, and clinging to a "tradition." They fail to realize that the judges who presided over Galileo's case were not the only people who held to a geocentric view of the universe. It was the received view among scientists at the time. Centuries earlier, Aristotle had refuted heliocentrism, and by Galileo's time, nearly every major thinker subscribed to a geocentric view. Copernicus refrained from publishing his heliocentric theory for some time, not out of fear of censure from the Church but out of fear of ridicule from his colleagues.

Many people wrongly believe Galileo proved heliocentrism. He could not answer the strongest argument against it, which had been made nearly two thousand years earlier by Aristotle: If heliocentrism were true, then there would be observable parallax shifts in the stars' positions as the earth moved in its orbit around the sun. However, given the technology of Galileo's time, no such shifts in their positions could be observed. It would require more sensitive measuring equipment than was available in Galileo's day to document the existence of these shifts, given the stars' great distance. Until then, the available evidence suggested that the stars were fixed in their positions relative to the earth, and, thus, that the earth and the stars were not moving in space—only the sun, moon, and planets were. Most astronomers in that day were not convinced of the great distance of the stars that the Copernican theory required to account for the absence of observable parallax shifts. This is one of the main reasons why the respected astronomer Tycho Brahe refused to adopt Copernicus fully.

Galileo could have safely proposed heliocentrism as a theory or a method to more simply account for the planets' motions. His problem arose when he stopped proposing it as a scientific theory and began proclaiming it as truth, though there was no conclusive proof of it at the time. Even so, Galileo would not have been in so much trouble if he had chosen to stay within the realm of science and out of the realm of theology.

In 1614, Galileo felt compelled to answer the charge that this "new science" was contrary to certain Scripture passages. His opponents pointed to Bible passages with statements like, "And the sun stood still, and the moon stayed . . ." (Josh. 10:13). This is not an isolated occurrence. Psalms 93 and 104 and Ecclesiastes 1:5 also speak of celestial motion and terrestrial stability. A literalistic reading of these passages would have to be abandoned if the heliocentric theory were adopted. Yet this should not have posed a problem. As Augustine put it, "One does not read in the Gospel that the Lord said: 'I will send you the Paraclete who will teach you about the course of the sun and moon.' For he willed to make them Christians, not mathematicians." Following Augustine's example, Galileo urged caution in not interpreting these biblical statements too literally.

Unfortunately, throughout Church history, there have been those who insist on reading the Bible in a more literal sense than it was intended. They fail to appreciate, for example, instances in which Scripture uses what is called "phenomenological" language—that is, the language of appearances. Just as we today speak of the sun rising and setting to cause day and night, rather than the earth turning, so did the ancients. From an earthbound perspective, the sun does appear to rise and appear to set, and the earth appears to be immobile. When we describe these things according to their appearances, we are using phenomenological language.

The phenomenological language concerning the motion of the heavens and the non-motion of the earth is obvious to us today but was less so in previous centuries. Scripture scholars of the past were willing to consider whether particular statements were to be taken literally or phenomenologically, but they did not like being told by a non-Scripture scholar, such as Galileo, that the words of the sacred page must be taken in a particular sense.

During this period, personal interpretation of Scripture was a sensitive subject. In the early 1600s, the Church had just been through the Reformation experience, and one of the chief quarrels with Protestants was over individual interpretation of the Bible.

Theologians were not prepared to entertain the heliocentric theory based on a layman's interpretation. There is little question that if Galileo had kept the discussion within the accepted boundaries of astronomy (i.e., predicting planetary motions) and had not claimed physical truth for the heliocentric theory, the issue would not have escalated to the point it did. After all, he had not proved the new theory beyond reasonable doubt.

Galileo "Confronts" Rome

Galileo came to Rome to see Pope Paul V (r. 1605-1621). The pope turned the matter over to the Holy Office, which issued a condemnation of Galileo's theory in 1616. Things returned to relative quiet for a time, until Galileo forced another showdown.

At Galileo's request, Cardinal Robert Bellarmine, a Jesuit—one of the most important Catholic theologians of the day—issued a certificate that, although it forbade Galileo to hold or defend the heliocentric theory, did not prevent him from conjecturing it. When Galileo met with the new pope, Urban VIII, in 1623, he received permission from his longtime friend to write a work on heliocentrism, but the new pontiff cautioned him not to advocate the new position, only to present arguments for and against it. When Galileo wrote the *Dialogue on the Two World Systems*, he used an argument the pope had offered and placed it in the mouth of his character Simplicio. Galileo had mocked the very person he needed as a benefactor. He also alienated his long-time supporters, the Jesuits, with attacks on one of their astronomers. The result was the infamous trial, which is still heralded as the final separation of science and religion.

Tortured for His Beliefs?

In the end, Galileo recanted his heliocentric teachings, but it was not—as is commonly supposed—under torture, nor after a harsh imprisonment. Galileo was, in fact, treated surprisingly well.

As historian Giorgio de Santillana, who is not overly fond of the Catholic Church, noted, "We must, if anything, admire the cautiousness and legal scruples of the Roman authorities." Galileo was offered every convenience possible to make his imprisonment in his home bearable.

Galileo's friend Nicolini, Tuscan ambassador to the Vatican, sent regular reports to the court regarding affairs in Rome. Nicolini revealed the circumstances surrounding Galileo's "imprisonment" when he reported to the Tuscan king: "The pope told me that he had shown Galileo a favor never accorded to another" (letter dated Feb. 13, 1633); "he has a servant and every convenience" (letter, April 16); and "the pope says that after the publication of the sentence he will consider with me as to what can be done to afflict him as little as possible" (letter, June 18).

While instruments of torture may have been present during Galileo's recantation (this was the custom of the legal system in Europe at that time), they definitely were not used. The records demonstrate that Galileo could not be tortured because of regulations laid down in The Directory for Inquisitors (Nicholas Eymeric, 1595). This was the official guide of the Holy Office, the Church office charged with dealing with such matters, and was followed to the letter.

As noted scientist and philosopher Alfred North Whitehead remarked, in an age that saw a large number of "witches" subjected to torture and execution by Protestants in New England, "the worst that happened to the men of science was that Galileo suffered an honorable detention and a mild reproof."

Infallibility

Although three of the ten cardinals who judged Galileo refused to sign the verdict, his works were eventually condemned. Anti-

Catholics often assert that his conviction and later rehabilitation somehow disproves the doctrine of papal infallibility, but this is not the case, for the pope never tried to make an infallible ruling concerning Galileo's views.

The Church has never claimed ordinary tribunals, such as the one that judged Galileo, to be infallible. Church tribunals have disciplinary and juridical authority only; neither they nor their decisions are infallible. No ecumenical council met concerning Galileo, and the pope was not at the center of the discussions, which were handled by the Holy Office. When the Holy Office finished its work, Urban VIII ratified its verdict but did not attempt to engage infallibility. Three conditions must be met for a pope to exercise the charism of infallibility: (1) he must speak in his official capacity as the successor of Peter; (2) he must speak on a matter of faith or morals; and (3) he must solemnly define the doctrine as one that must be held by all the faithful.

In Galileo's case, the second and third conditions were not present, and possibly not even the first. Catholic theology has never claimed that a mere papal ratification of a tribunal decree is an exercise of infallibility. It is a straw man argument to represent the Catholic Church as having infallibly defined a scientific theory that turned out to be false. The strongest claim that can be made is that the Church of Galileo's day issued a non-infallible disciplinary ruling concerning a scientist who was advocating a new and still-unproven theory and demanding that the Church change its understanding of Scripture to fit his.

It is a good thing that the Church did not rush to embrace Galileo's views, because it turned out that his ideas were not entirely correct, either. Galileo believed that the sun was not just the fixed center of the solar system but the fixed center of the universe. We now know that the sun is not the center of the universe and that it does move—it simply orbits the center of the galaxy rather than the earth. Had the Catholic Church rushed to endorse Galileo's views—and there were many in the Church who were quite favorable to them—the Church would have embraced what modern science has disproved.

Fraud in Science Cannot Be Tolerated in Any Country

Jiefu Huang, Xinting Sang, and Shouxian Zhong

The authors are affiliated with the Department of Liver Surgery, Peking Union Medical College Hospital in Beijing, China.

On April 20, 2017, *Tumor Biology* of Springer announced to retract 107 articles with peer-review fraud, mostly authored by more than 500 scientists from well-known universities and top hospitals in China. With its highest proportion and largest amount of involved papers, this scandal is the worst academic fraud in recent years in China, raising public outcry. Pitifully, this event is just like a breeze that only ripples the water, causing no storm nor shake in the pond of Chinese scientific and technologic circles, under which flushes the undercurrent of fickleness and greed. What's more incredible, some official websites respond with no efforts in the reflection and renovation in academy, but spearhead their attacks at the publishing company. They question the review system of the journal, and even complain about the injustice to the fraud makers by claiming that the title evaluation system pushes the doctors to abandon their moral compass and therefore the academic fraud is excusable. We notice that even the administrative department of the science and technology is partial to fraud makers, much cry and little done. This is deplorable.

Academic fraud is always a harm to scientific research. In recent years, cheat in academy is increasing in our country. If there is no exhaustive investigation, it will become an incurable disease which will seriously impede the realization of a scientific power. Countries around the world have been serious about such scandals. In 2005, the "Pride of Korea," Woo-suk Hwang, faked data in his paper, and ended up with his dismissal from all the

"A Call for Scientific Integrity," by Jiefu Huang, Xinting Sang, and Shouxian Zhong, AME Publishing Company, May 19, 2017. Reprinted by permission.

posts. This "national hero" was brought down from the pedestal since then. In 2014, Japanese scientist Haruko Obokata fabricated STAP cell research. She was finally forced to resign and lost her Doctor's degree, and her supervisor, also the co-author of the paper, Yoshiki Sasai, hanged himself under great pressure, and all the people involved in Haruko Obokata's degree were severely punished. The two neighboring countries show tough attitudes toward scientific swindle, shouldn't we follow the example?

China is on the great journey of "national rejuvenation." Scientific and technological innovation is the base of a powerful country, and requires seeking truth from facts, allowing no dishonesty, especially academic misconduct. Confucius said: "If the people have no faith in their rulers, there is no standing for the state." Integrity is the foundation of a country. China has a long history of credibility culture, and the dream of development and a strong nation is based on its people's persistent self-improvement. The achievement of atomic and hydrogen bombs and man-made satellites, as well as the recent flight and launch of CA919 and Type 001A aircraft carriers, is made by Chinese people's ingenuity and industriousness. Lured by the lust of position promotion, awards, fame and wealth, academic fakers throw away scientists' professional ethics and integrity, purchase papers, falsify data, and publish their articles in foreign magazines. This fatal misconduct severely damages China's reputation. If this can be tolerated, what cannot?

Academic fraud and favoritism will result in a huge waste of educational and scientific research resources, and lead the scientific efforts to a wrong direction. In 2003, Professor Jin Chen of Shanghai Jiao Tong University faked chips, bringing a huge loss to China's science and technology. Isn't this thought-provoking? If the unhealthy tendency of faking cannot be stopped, greed and desire will be rampant in scientific circles, faked papers will become a gate pass for fame seekers, and the strategic target of "rejuvenate the country through science and technology" will be buried in oblivion.

China's reform and opening-up is developing vigorously, and senior government leaders, with decisive resolution, are leading people to push social and economic development. The unprecedentedly severe anti-corruption policy aims to crack down both tigers and flies. In 2016 in Liaoning Province, 454 Representatives of the Provincial People's Congress were involved in bribery in the election. President Jinping Xi strongly rebuked these illegal activities, and central government carried out a strict investigation. Four provincial level officials were put into jail. Other representatives were subjective to the Party disciplines and state laws and forfeited the right to represent the people. No excuse and compromise for corruption, isn't this a good example? We hope the national department of science and technology can erect their back straight and be tough and resolute. Scientific misconduct should be punished severely, academic management should be normalized, and fraud makers should be cleaned out from research teams. And there should be credit records and big data for scientists to ensure transparent scientific research. The academic field calls for breakthrough, the existing title evaluation system of science and education requires eliminating vice and exalting virtue, and the administrative system needs thorough reform. Only this can establish a healthy academic environment, and make the diligent and honest scientist raise their heads up to stand on the international scientific stage.

We hope our peers with the same belief can remember the Hippocratic Oath: "I will use treatment to help the sick according to my ability and judgment, but never with a view to injury and wrong-doing." Be faithful, perseverant, and dedicated. Integrity is self-cultivation, generosity, a state of mind and a great spirit, which is the essence of a real life. We should practice honesty to demonstrate our personality, and integrate this virtue into the national spirit to realize the great rejuvenation of China.

Organizations to Contact

The editors have compiled the following list of organizations concerned with the issues debated in this book. The descriptions are derived from materials provided by the organizations. All have publications or information available for interested readers. This list was compiled on the date of publication of the present volume; the information provided here may change. Be aware that many organizations take several weeks or longer to respond to inquiries, so allow as much time as possible.

American Association for the Advancement of Science (AAAS)
1200 New York Avenue NW
Washington, DC 20005
(202) 326-6400
website: www.aaas.org

AAAS is an organization that has one mission: to advance engineering, science, and innovation throughout the world, so that all people will benefit. The website includes up-to-date science articles and a link giving information about science careers.

Future of Life Institute
PO Box 706
Brighton, MA 02135
website: www.futureoflife.org

The Future Life Institute is a charity and outreach organization. The group works to ensure that powerful technology stays as a beneficial force for all people. Its work focuses on protecting AI and reducing the risks of biotechnology and nuclear technology.

Japanese Science and Technology Agency (JST)
2001 L Street NW
Suite 1050
Washington, DC 20036
(202) 728-0007
website: www.jst.go.jp/EN/

JST plays a vital role in the science and technology of Japan. The organization plays a role based on governmental ideas, which includes research and development, future technology, and education.

Massachusetts Institute of Technology (MIT)
77 Massachusetts Avenue
Cambridge, MA 02139
(617) 253-1000
website: www.mit.edu/

MIT is an educational institution dedicated to providing students with the knowledge in science and technology to serve both the United States and the world.

National Academy of Sciences (NAS)
500 Fifth Street NW
Washington, DC 20001-2101
(202) 334-2000
website: www.nationalacademies.org/home

NAS is an organization dedicated to science, medicine, and engineering. This large group sparks education to achieve the best in science, engineering, and medicine for the US.

National Aeronautics and Space Administration
300 E. Street SW, Suite 5R30
Washington, DC 20546
(202) 358-0001
website: www.nasa.gov/

NASA maintains a vast site providing information in a variety of formats on a huge range of science topics. Individuals can download materials, view photos, listen to podcasts, and much more.

National Center for Science Education (NCSE)
1904 Franklin Street
Suite 600
Oakland, CA 94612
(510) 601-7203
email: info@ncse.ngo
website: www.ncse.ngo

NCSE is committed to achieving world class science education for all students. It actively resolves issues where sound science education is being targeted, blocked, or attacked.

National Science Foundation (NSF)
2415 Eisenhower Avenue
Alexandria, VA 22314
(703) 292-5111
email: info@nsf.gov
website: www.nsf.gov

NSF has a mission to support all fundamental science and engineering in the United States. It works to keep the US on the frontiers of discovery in science and engineering.

Union of Concerned Scientists (UCS)
2 Brattle Square
Cambridge, MA 02138
(617) 547-5552
website: www.ucsusa.org/

UCS is dedicated to using rigorous, independent science to solve the planet's problems. This organization backs research, fights misinformation, defends science, and mobilizes people to seek change.

Bibliography

Books

Melissa Abramovitz. *Stem Cells*. New York, NY: Lucent Books, 2012.

Nick Bostrom. *Superintelligence: Paths, Dangers, Strategies*. Oxford, UK: Oxford University Press, 2014.

Ann C. Cunningham. *Artificial Intelligence and the Technological Singularity*. New York, NY: Greenhaven Press, 2017.

Louise Gerdes. *Human Genetics*. New York, NY: Greenhaven Press, 2014.

John Grant. *Eureka! 50 Scientists Who Shaped Human History*. Minneapolis, MN: Zest Books, 2016.

Tara Haelle. *Vaccinations Investigation: The History and Science of Vaccines*. Minneapolis, MN: Twenty-First Century Books, 2018.

Peter J. Hotez. *Vaccines Did Not Cause Rachel's Autism: My Journey as a Vaccine Scientist, Pediatrician, and Autism Dad*. Baltimore, MD: Johns Hopkins University Press. 2018.

Sheldon Krimsky. *GMOs Decoded: A Skeptic's View of Genetically Modified Foods*. Cambridge, MA: MIT Press, 2019.

Stephanie Sammartino McPherson. *Artificial Intelligence: Building Smarter Machines*. Minneapolis, MN: Twenty-First Century Books, 2018.

Noel Merino. *Vaccines*. New York, NY: Greenhaven Press, 2012.

Michael Miller. *Fake News: Separating Truth from Fiction*. Minneapolis, MN: Twenty-First Century Books, 2018.

Don Nardo. *How Vaccines Changed the World.* San Diego, CA: Reference Point Press Inc., 2019.

Bill Nye. *Undeniable: Evolution and the Science of Creation.* New York, NY: St. Martin's Press, 2014.

Paul A. Offit. *Pandora's Lab: Seven Stories of Science Gone Wrong.* New York, NY: National Geographic Partners LLC, 2017.

Linda Barrett Osborne. *Guardians of Liberty: Freedom of the Press and the Nature of News.* New York, NY: Abrams Books for Young Readers, 2020.

Daniel T. Willingham. *When Can You Trust the Experts? How to Tell Good Science from Bad in Education.* San Francisco, CA: Jossey-Bass, 2012.

H. P. Wood. *Fakers: An Insider's Guide to Cons, Hoaxes, and Scams.* Watertown, MA: Charlesbridge, 2018.

Periodicals and Internet Sources

Timothy Caulfield, "Pseudoscience and Covid-19—We've Had Enough Already," *Nature*, April 27, 2020. https://www.nature.com/articles/d41586-020-01266-z.

Rory Cellan-Jones, "Stephen Hawking Warns Artificial Intelligence Could End Mankind," BBC News, December 2, 2014. https://www.bbc.com/news/technology-30290540.

Nic Fleming, "Coronavirus Misinformation, and How Scientists Can Help to Fight It," *Nature*, June 17, 2020. https://www.nature.com/articles/d41586-020-01834-3.

Jan Hoffman, "A Call to Arms: Under Attack, Pro-Vaccine Doctors Fight Back," *New York Times*, March 10, 2020. https://www.nytimes.com/2020/03/10/health/vaccines-protest-doctors.html.

Nicoletta Lanese, "'Crazymothers' Want You to Stop Calling Them 'Anti-Vaxxers,'" Live Science, December 4, 2019.

https://www.livescience.com/anti-vaxxers-try-to-change
-name.html.

Tanya Lewis, "Stephen Hawking Thinks These 3 Things Could Destroy Humanity," Live Science, February 26, 2015. https:// www.livescience.com/49952-stephen-hawking-warnings-to -humanity.html.

Daniel Mollenkamp, "Tracking the Anti-Science Wave: Commentary on the Roots of Mistrust," *Christian Science Monitor*, July 31, 2020. https://www.csmonitor.com /Commentary/2020/0731/Tracking-the-anti-science -wave-Commentary-on-the-roots-of-distrust.

Dana Nuccitelli, "Fake News Is a Threat to Humanity, But Scientists May Have a Solution," *Guardian*, December 27, 2017. https://www.theguardian.com/environment/climate -consensus-97-per-cent/2017/dec/27/fake-news-is-a-threat -to-humanity-but-scientists-may-have-a-solution.

Maria Temming, "Scientists Enlist Computers to Hunt Down Fake News," Science News for Students, September 27, 2018. https://www.sciencenewsforstudents.org/article/scientists -enlist-computers-hunt-down-fake-news.

Dan Vergano, "Galileo Matters More Than Ever on His 450th Birthday," *National Geographic*, February 16, 2014. https:// www.nationalgeographic.com/news/2014/2/140215-galileo -450-birthday-appreciation-science-history/.

Jessica Wolf, "The Truth About Galileo and His Conflict with the Catholic Church," UCLA Newsroom, December 22, 2016. https://newsroom.ucla.edu/releases/the-truth-about -galileo-and-his-conflict-with-the-catholic-church.

Index

5